THIS BOOK
BELONGS TO

_____

A LITTLE
GOD
TIME
FOR
teens

BroadStreet
PUBLISHING

BroadStreet Publishing Group LLC
Savage, Minnesota, USA
Broadstreetpublishing.com

A LITTLE GOD TIME FOR TEENS

978-1-4245-6041-7 (faux)
978-1-4245-5208-5 (e-book)

Devotional entries composed by Cari Dugan, Claire Flores, Laura Krause, Cate Mezyk, and Stephanie Sample.

Design by Chris Garborg | garborgdesign.com
Edited and compiled by Michelle Winger | literallyprecise.com

Printed in China.

20   21   22   23   24   25   6   5   4   3   2   1

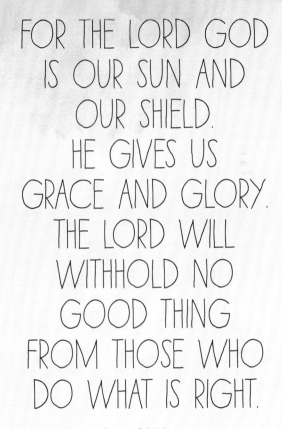

FOR THE LORD GOD
IS OUR SUN AND
OUR SHIELD.
HE GIVES US
GRACE AND GLORY.
THE LORD WILL
WITHHOLD NO
GOOD THING
FROM THOSE WHO
DO WHAT IS RIGHT.

PSALM 84:11 NLT

INTRODUCTION

This devotional is written specifically
for teenage girls—like you! It will engage
you in topics specific to the issues you
face each day. Read about themes
like beauty, courage, dignity, identity,
integrity, and value, and be encouraged
to find everything you need in Christ!

Gain confidence as you learn that
the God who created you delights in
spending time with you. As you embrace
his words of truth, be filled with joy,
strength, and renewed purpose for the
day ahead.

JANUARY

Before he made the world, God chose us to
be his very own through what Christ would
do for us; he decided then to make us holy in
his eyes, without a single fault—we who stand
before him covered with his love.

EPHESIANS 1:4 TLB

BUILT ON PURPOSE

It was you who formed my inward parts;
you knit me together in my mother's womb.
I praise you, for I am fearfully and wonderfully made.
Wonderful are your works;
that I know very well.

PSALM 139:13-14 NRSV

Even before you were born, the Lord was busy working on you. God knew what color your eyes were going to be, and how thick or thin or curly or straight your hair would turn out. And even better, he knew all the character traits that add up to exactly what makes you, you!

Here's the best thing: God doesn't make mistakes. What does that mean for you? It means that he knew what he was doing with every trait he gave you. He thinks you are wonderful! You may be questioning why you were born with such and such, or why you have this or that personality trait. But he built you that way on purpose, to use it for his glory, because he saw the beauty in it!

Lord, help me to see how wonderfully you've made me, each and every day.

TEST OF TIME

"People are like grass;
their beauty is like a flower in the field.
The grass withers and the flower fades.
But the word of the Lord remains forever."
And that word is the Good News that was preached to you.

1 PETER 1:24-25 NLT

When you are in the middle of troubling times, it can feel like it's going to last forever. The teenage years can feel like one big competition. Who is the most popular? When will the school record for such and such be broken? Who is wearing what, and who is going out with whom? There's intense pressure to keep up with it all.

Take heart, and be encouraged. There is nothing wrong with being popular or succeeding, but it isn't enduring. The Bible tells us earthly things are like the flowers of the field. They're beautiful while they last, but they fade away. What's left to stand the test of time is the Word of the Lord. Stand on that truth when the pressure begins to build in your life.

Lord, I pray that I would see past the glories of the here and now and instead see what's enduring. Help me to stand on your truth when pressure threatens to get to me.

HE HAS MY BACK

What shall we say about such wonderful things as these? If God is for us, who can ever be against us?

ROMANS 8:31 NLT

Sometimes it feels like the whole world is out to get you. Even your friends can't identify with you at times. But there is one who always understands you. One who grasps exactly who you are, right down to the depths of your soul. When it seems like the rest of the world is pitted against you, God is always for you, rooting for you, and on your side.

Doesn't it feel good to know that you are never alone? You've always got someone to turn to, no matter how big your problems may seem. It's amazing how just knowing that someone has your back can turn things around.

Lord, thank you for being there for me. I praise you for being the one I can turn to in my every moment of need, regardless of the circumstance. Since you are for me, who can be against me? I pray I'd look to you when I'm feeling alone, and that I'd remember that someone always has my back.

SUBMISSION

*Submit therefore to God. Resist the
devil and he will flee from you.*

JAMES 4:7 NASB

One of the hardest things to do in life is to submit to
someone else's authority. Giving up control sounds like
a terrible idea! We want complete jurisdiction over the
decisions we make, right? And yet, we're asked to give that
up. As believers in Christ, we are told that we need to give
our lives over to him.

Submission means to yield to another person. In Christ's
case, he is superior to us in every way, shape, and form.
Although he is superior, and though he could have forced
us all into submission, he has given us the choice. We can
choose to live a better life through him, full of wisdom and
joy, or we can choose otherwise. He loves us enough to let
us decide.

*Lord, I pray I'd choose daily to submit myself to you. Give
me wisdom in my decisions and the joy that comes from
knowing you in a deep and real way. Thank you for giving
me the choice, and for loving me so well.*

DON'T BE STUPID

Whoever loves discipline loves knowledge,
but whoever hates correction is stupid.
PROVERBS 12:1 NIV

Sometimes things need to be said in plain English. That's what is so great about Proverbs. It's a book that tells it like it is. Proverbs says that hating correction is just plain stupid.

Nobody likes to look stupid. On the other hand, taking correction can be an incredibly difficult thing to do. And discipline? Well, that doesn't seem like much fun.

Discipline is what we need in order to grow spiritually. We need to be corrected when we are living under a false assumption or making the same mistake time and time again. It's good for us to be disciplined, especially when it's done in love. So while it may not be fun, it's what's best for our lives.

Lord, thank you for your discipline. You are loving in all that you do, and your gentle corrections are no different. Thank you that you don't allow me to go about my days making mistakes without accountability. Instead, you step in and let me know when I've done wrong. I pray I'd take your instruction and the instruction of others with a grateful heart.

WORDS WITH ACTION

*My children, we should love people not only with
words and talk, but by our actions and true caring.*
1 John 3:18 NCV

We've all seen people who preach about what Christians
should be doing but don't apply it to their own lives.
Perhaps they shout it in all caps on social media, but there's
no love behind their words.

The fact is you can talk all day long about what it means
to be a Christian, but without action, it's meaningless. A
better approach is to show love to Christ by putting faith
into action. Serve others around you. Stand up for what's
true. Treat people with kindness and put them first. Give
selflessly. Your words are only a part of how you're called to
live differently. Look around you for ways that you put your
love into action.

*Lord, I know that there are many ways I can live out your
love here on earth. Open my eyes to see how I can serve
others and show your love to the people around me. Help
me to live as an example of your truth.*

LETTING GO

*Bearing with one another, and forgiving one another,
if anyone has a complaint against another; even
as Christ forgave you, so you also must do.*

COLOSSIANS 3:13 NKJV

When someone hurts you, it can be really tough to let go of your frustration and forgive that person. Everything in you wants to maintain a firm grip on anger. *It's not fair,* you might think. *It's not right!* You want to hold on to the injustice of it all. But the Lord created forgiveness as a way to relieve a burden. Hanging on to that hardness of your heart is like hanging on to a pile a bricks that needlessly weigh you down.

Forgiving isn't easy. And letting go of your anger and hurt doesn't mean you're saying that what happened was okay. But when you stop being resentful it's as good for you as it is for the one you're forgiving. You may be surprised to find that you actually feel lighter after you've figured out how to let it go.

Lord, help me to forgive others like you've forgiven me. Forgive me for any resentment I've had. Relieve me of any burden I've carried in my resentment. I pray I'd be able to move on and let go.

LIFTED IN PRAYER

Confess your sins to one another and pray for one another, that you may be healed. The prayer of a righteous person has great power as it is working.

JAMES 5:16 ESV

One of the greatest gifts the Lord has ever given us is the community we have with other Christians. Friends who also love Jesus keep us accountable for our actions. We can turn to them in times of trouble and be lifted up in prayer.

The Lord wants each of us to spend time in prayer on our own, but there is something special and powerful about praying with others. When we come together, asking God for something in unity, amazing things happen. Not only are prayers answered, we're drawn together in a deeper way than we'd ever thought possible. When we allow ourselves to be vulnerable in this way, it pulls us together and our relationship with God will grow.

Lord, thank you for the gift of friendship. It's an incredible blessing to be prayed over and in turn to pray for others. Help me to ask for prayer when I'm in need.

DEPTH OF FEELING

Jesus wept.
JOHN 11:35 NIV

It's the shortest verse in the Bible, and yet these two words say so much. They tell us that the God we serve is one who understands us. He gets where we are coming from because he's been there. He has experienced everything we have because he humbled himself to become human. He has intimate knowledge of just how we feel.

When Jesus felt sorrow, he wept. Weeping doesn't mean a little sniffle and an "I'm sort of sad" shrug of the shoulders. Weeping can bring you to your knees; it's a deeply felt kind of misery. When it seems like there isn't anyone else who understands how you feel, picture Jesus weeping, and know that you are never alone. There is someone who gets you.

Lord, thank you for the ways in which you truly understand me. I know that I can turn to you because you grasp just how I am feeling in every situation. I love how you love me.

JOY OF SALVATION

Restore to me the joy of your salvation,
and sustain in me a willing spirit.
PSALM 51:12 NRSV

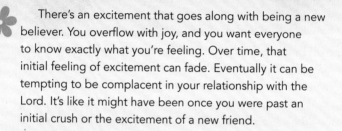

There's an excitement that goes along with being a new believer. You overflow with joy, and you want everyone to know exactly what you're feeling. Over time, that initial feeling of excitement can fade. Eventually it can be tempting to be complacent in your relationship with the Lord. It's like it might have been once you were past an initial crush or the excitement of a new friend.

Sometimes you need to pray for protection over your relationship with the Lord. Pray that you'd come back to the same eagerness and enthusiasm you had at the beginning. Your relationship with God is meant to go the distance, not simmer hot then fizzle out. As you grow in your spiritual life, you'll learn more and more. That growth will sustain you for the long run.

Lord, thank you for the joy of your salvation. I want our relationship to grow strong and deep.

NO WORDS

In the same way, the Spirit helps us in our weakness. We
do not know what we ought to pray for, but the Spirit
himself intercedes for us through wordless groans.

ROMANS 8:26 NIV

Ever feel like you want to pray, but you have no clue
what to say? Guess what? Even when you have no idea what
to say, it doesn't matter! God's Spirit is always with you,
helping you along. When your mouth opens, but you freeze
up and no words come out, he fills in the gaps and gives
you the words to say. If your heart is willing, he does the
praying for you.

He knows you better than you know yourself. He cares
about every detail, even when it comes to the words you
pray. So you never have to worry. Just place yourself in his
presence, and the rest will come.

Lord, thank you for filling in the gaps for me when I have no
idea what to say. I praise you for knowing me so well. Help
me to be open to your presence today and every day.

WISDOM AT EVERY TURN

If you are wise and understand God's ways, prove it by living an honorable life, doing good works with the humility that comes from wisdom.

JAMES 3:13 NLT

When you think of a wise person, is there anyone specific who comes to mind? What is it about that person that makes you think they are so wise? Certain qualities define a wise person. How they live their lives and *show* wisdom is the most important quality of all. It's more than talk; it's their walk. Boasting about their greatness or knowledge doesn't do it. Twisting situations to put themselves in a better light certainly doesn't either.

But living a life that follows the example Christ set is a great way to become wise. When we are humble, ask for others' opinions, seek knowledge, and live to serve, we find wisdom for ourselves. Be wise and follow the Lord!

Father, thank you for being the ultimate giver of wisdom. I want to seek your wisdom at every turn. I pray that I'd resist the temptation to tell people how knowledgeable I am. I pray I'd remain your humble servant.

STRENGTH TO TURN AWAY

We do not have a high priest who is unable to sympathize with our weaknesses, but one who in every respect has been tempted as we are, yet without sin.

HEBREWS 4:15 ESV

Do you ever feel like the Bible just doesn't apply to modern life? Or that God doesn't understand because he's a distant God who couldn't possibly get what's going on in your life? After all, you're faced with daily temptations, and there he is, up in heaven, unable to see what you're going through.

Here's the thing: God went through it all himself. The clothing styles may have been different and the technology certainly wasn't there, but Jesus Christ came to earth and faced the same things you do today. Greed, jealousy, lust—he saw it all. So he really does understand. Jesus knows what you're facing, because he faced it too—and won. You can look temptation in the eye and beat it, because you have Jesus in your life.

Lord, thank you for your empathy. Thanks for understanding where I am and walking through many of the same temptations yourself. Give me the strength to turn away from temptation today.

WISDOM IN WORDS

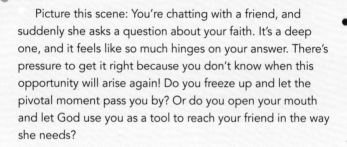

*Be wise in the way you act toward outsiders; make
the most of every opportunity. Let your conversation
be always full of grace, seasoned with salt, so
that you may know how to answer everyone.*

COLOSSIANS 4:5-6 NIV

Picture this scene: You're chatting with a friend, and
suddenly she asks a question about your faith. It's a deep
one, and it feels like so much hinges on your answer. There's
pressure to get it right because you don't know when this
opportunity will arise again! Do you freeze up and let the
pivotal moment pass you by? Or do you open your mouth
and let God use you as a tool to reach your friend in the way
she needs?

The Lord will give you wisdom in every situation if you
are open to it. He will give you the words to say, even when
you have no idea what they are. Let him use you to reach
those around you!

*Father, I pray that you will use me in conversation with my
friends. I pray I'd make the most of every opportunity that
arises, and that my friendships would become my personal
mission field. Thank you for giving me wisdom when I don't
have the words to say on my own.*

ALREADY SELECTED

*You are a chosen generation, a royal priesthood,
a holy nation, His own special people, that you
may proclaim the praises of Him who called you
out of darkness into His marvelous light.*

1 PETER 2:9 NKJV

Remember in school when you divide into groups, and slowly the captains select people for their team? For someone who isn't picked early on, the waiting can seem like forever. No one wants to be the last one picked. Guess what? God has already chosen you for his team. He picked you, right away, with no hesitation. He even calls you his special possession!

The rules of the game are simple: believe in him, follow his Word, speak out for him, do his work, and share his love with others. Tell everyone you know about the ways he has changed you for the better. He wants as many people as possible on his team, and he's calling you to add those members.

Lord, I praise you for all you've done for me. I pray I'd have the courage to be an active team member for your kingdom, sharing your love.

YOU BELONG

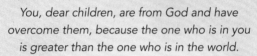

*You, dear children, are from God and have
overcome them, because the one who is in you
is greater than the one who is in the world.*

1 John 4:4 NIV

Do you ever feel like you just don't belong anywhere?
You might feel you don't fit in and that no one truly cares
for you. That's a lie that the enemy wants you to believe.
The truth is you are created by God. If you've put your faith
in him, he lives in you and cares for you. And that means
you belong. You belong to the best team you could ever
imagine. It's the team that wins, and the team that's been
formed out of love.

When you feel like an outsider, remember that you've
been handpicked to be a part of the best. God wants you
as an integral member of his team, and his Holy Spirit is in
you, urging you on to victory over those that would bring
you down.

*Lord, thank you for choosing me for your team. I know I am
created by you, and you are in me. I'm simply in awe.*

PARTY INVITATION

*We through the Spirit, by faith, are waiting
for the hope of righteousness.*
GALATIANS 5:5 NASB

When you were little did you ever have anything that you couldn't wait to happen? Like a best friend's sleepover or a birthday party? How many times did you ask, "How much longer," or "When will it be time to go?" You just couldn't wait to get there, and the minutes ahead of time felt interminable.

There's an exciting party happening soon, and we're living in anticipation of its starting time. The theme of this party is righteousness, and it'll be the most happening event in heaven. It's not an exclusive party. God wants to invite anyone and everyone. And as long as we live in faith, we've got an invitation.

Father, I cannot wait for the party you'll be throwing in heaven. I pray that I'd see the faces of everyone I know there too, and that my life would serve as an invitation to others to join the fun.

INDWELLING

A person who does not have the Spirit does not accept the truths that come from the Spirit of God. That person thinks they are foolish and cannot understand them, because they can only be judged to be true by the Spirit.

1 Corinthians 2:14 NCV

If you met someone on the street and they said, "There's this guy that wants to live inside you and change your life," you'd probably run in the opposite direction. At the very least, it sounds a little goofy, doesn't it? And yet, it's true. There is someone who wants to take up residence within you! The person will give you the greatest joy you've ever known.

The Lord has given those who believe in him an incredible gift—his Holy Spirit. He's the one who resides with us and within us. He gives us the wisdom, knowledge, and power we wouldn't otherwise have without him. We can turn to him at any time.

Lord, I praise you today for the gift of your Holy Spirit. I know that without this gift, my life just wouldn't be the same. I'm thankful for it!

TEMPLE OF GOD

Do you not know that your bodies are temples of the Holy Spirit, who is in you, whom you have received from God? You are not your own; you were bought at a price. Therefore honor God with your bodies.

1 CORINTHIANS 6:19-20 NIV

When we accept Jesus Christ as our Savior, we are asking him to enter our lives and lead us in everything we say and do. As we mature spiritually, we walk closer and closer to him, making wise decisions in our daily choices. So why is it that we often forget that self-care is a part of that? So many times we choose to obey the Lord in other areas of our lives but forget one of the most important things—caring for ourselves.

God created us and formed us in his image. If *he* cares about us, *we* should care about us! That means getting enough sleep, eating healthy foods, exercising, and not giving our bodies to anyone or anything else that would displease him. He tells us that our bodies are his temples, and we should care for them as if they are worthy of that distinction.

Father, thank you for creating me. Help me to take good care of your temple.

ANOTHER MIRROR

If any are hearers of the word and not doers, they are like those who look at themselves in a mirror; for they look at themselves and, on going away, immediately forget what they were like. But those who look into the perfect law, the law of liberty, and persevere, being not hearers who forget but doers who act—they will be blessed in their doing.

JAMES 1:23-25 NRSV

Before you leave your house every day, you look in the mirror, right? You check to see that your hair isn't out of place, or that you don't have any crumbs on your face, or that your clothes look ok. But there's another mirror you want to be looking in daily, and it's often overlooked completely.

The book of James says you're a reflection of Christ in this world. He provides his Word, the Bible, for you as a way to learn how to be like him. It's his mirror. You can look into that mirror, see how he loves others, and see the ways you can reflect him.

Lord, I pray I'd turn to your Word for help and show others what you're like in all I do and say.

THE TRAP

The fear of man brings a snare,
But he who trusts in the LORD will be exalted.
PROVERBS 29:25 NASB

It's hard not to worry about what others will think of us. The opinions of our friends and family can mean a lot, and we don't want to appear any less than perfect in their eyes. Contemplating how our actions might come across can actually keep us from moving forward at times.

The Bible tells us that this is a snare. So don't fall into the trap! While we do need to go to others for good judgment, we ultimately want to look to Christ. When we avoid being wrapped up in the good opinion of others, we'll be kept safe. He will protect us. So be confident in the decisions you make, knowing that the opinion that matters is the Lord's. People's view of you may change as easily as the breeze blows, but God's view of you is unchanging. He loves you always.

Father, thank you for keeping me safe. Help me to look to you for my confidence instead of to others. You love me so well!

DEPENDABLE

"For I hold you by your right hand—
I, the LORD your God.
And I say to you,
'Don't be afraid. I am here to help you.'"

ISAIAH 41:13 NLT

Did you know that the Lord would never lie to you? He won't lie because everything about him is truth. So when he flat out says that you have nothing to fear because he will help you, those aren't empty words. They're a promise, and he will see it through because his words are truth.

If you're afraid, reach out your hand to the one who loves you. He's ready to take it with a firm, yet gentle, grip. God is ready to pull you up out of whatever has you down. There is no need to fear, no need to worry, and no need to panic. He has it all under control and is always available to you. Depend on him. You won't regret your choice!

Lord, I give you my hand. Take it in your firm grip and help me through. Thank you for your truth. I know you will not let me down!

TOP PRIORITY

*It is the L ORD your God you must follow, and
him you must revere. Keep his commands and
obey him; serve him and hold fast to him.*

DEUTERONOMY 13:4 NIV

What are you holding onto today? Is it fear? Hurt?
Brokenness? Are you looking to your friends for their
approval? Here's the thing: if you are not holding on to
Christ himself, whatever else you're grasping will eventually
slip from your grip. Hold on to him and only him, as if your
life depends on it—because it does!

There is only one God, and he loves you with fierceness
beyond comparison. He wants you to put him first and
follow his commands. Anything else that you've placed
above him in your list of priorities needs to be re-thought
and re-shifted. Put God at the top. Hold firmly on to him. He
will hold you, protecting and loving you.

*Father, thank you for loving me. I pray I'd always put you at
the top of my priority list. I want to hold on to you and your
great love and never let go.*

SHARED STRENGTH

Be strong in the Lord and in the strength of his power.

EPHESIANS 6:10 NRSV

There's no doubt about it. God is strong, and he wants you to be strong too. In fact, there is nothing that you can't overcome when you have him on your side. You'll find a fortitude and resilience that you didn't know existed, all because his power is inside in you. He is mighty and he will save you.

God's strength is offered to you as a gift. Take that gift and put it to good use. When you are weary, or don't believe that you can make it through your current situation, turn to him and know that his power will get you through. You can't always go through life on your own, and the good news is that you don't have to. He promises to be right by your side, encouraging you all the while, sharing his strength and might with the child he loves.

Father, thank you for your strength. I need it today! I pray that your power would come upon me, helping me through each day.

LIGHT OF TRUTH

*You are to live clean, innocent lives as children of
God in a dark world full of people who are crooked
and stubborn. Shine out among them like beacon
lights, holding out to them the Word of Life.
Then when Christ returns, how glad I will be that
my work among you was so worthwhile.*

PHILIPPIANS 2:15-16 TLB

You, my friend, shine like a star. If you've got the love of
Christ inside you, it's like a radiant beam that shines bright
for all to see. You just can't help it. Let that light continue to
sparkle by keeping close to God and following his Word of
life and truth.

Even though circumstances around you might seem
bleak, you stand out because you have Christ within you.
People are drawn to you because of it. If you hold tight to
the Lord's truth, his love and his light shine through you.
Everyone who sees you will see his light too!

*Father, I want to shine for you as a light. Thank you for your
Word of life!*

FOREVER NEW

My flesh and my heart may fail,
but God is the strength of my heart
and my portion forever.

PSALM 73:26 NIV

Getting old may seem a long way away, but eventually skin begins to wrinkle and hair starts to gray. Muscles and bones start to weaken, and working out gets less fun.

The exciting news is that even when earthly bodies might not be perfect, or even when you're just feeling tired, the Lord promises to refresh your soul and give you strength. It's like he makes you new inside. He gives you strength when you don't feel like you have any of your own. All you need to do is ask. As you begin to rely on him, you will find a reward in your relationship with him that you may not have expected.

Father, thank you for being my strength and for renewing my spirit. My body will eventually wear out, but my soul is forever new in you.

CHANGED FROM WITHIN

Do not be shaped by this world; instead be changed within by a new way of thinking. Then you will be able to decide what God wants for you; you will know what is good and pleasing to him and what is perfect.

ROMANS 12:12 NCV

We all want to fit in, don't we? That's because when we blend in, others won't see us as weird or different or unusual. Sometimes, though, as we try hard to fit in, we might find ourselves fitting in *too* much. So much that we may not even notice when our values slip and we become more like the world around us than like Jesus.

God's desire is to lift you up and bring out the best in you. So be careful not to get pulled down into poor choices and unwise decisions. God wants you to be changed for the better.

God, I want to be above the things of this world and keep my focus on you and your will for me. Change me from the inside out!

LIFE OF PEACE

Let the peace of Christ rule in your hearts, to which indeed you were called in one body. And be thankful.

<small>COLOSSIANS 3:15 ESV</small>

From the time most of us were little, we were taught to be kind, tell the truth, and help others. But there's another thing we're also called to do—live in peace with each other. After all, we're all part of the same body, the group of believers that makes up the family of God. Peace comes from knowing Christ and allowing him to rule our lives.

Though the little sentence about being thankful seems tacked on almost as an afterthought, it is anything but that. Thankfulness, instead of complaining, brings people together. Thankfulness to God brings us closer to God. We can be thankful for everything he has given us, for everything he has done, and for everything he is. Let gratitude for him fill your heart.

Lord, thank you for calling us to a life of peace. Help me to live that out in my life.

DON'T LOSE HEART

We do not lose heart. Though outwardly we are wasting away, yet inwardly we are being renewed day by day.
2 CORINTHIANS 4:16 NIV

"Don't lose heart." That can be tough to do. Feeling discouraged seems to come easily at times. Sometimes interactions with others can leave us feeling down. That weight can chip away at us, bit by bit. But God promises that if we turn to him, we'll be renewed and refreshed.

Sometimes it takes repeating something over and over until you believe it. So repeat this as often as you need to: "I will not be discouraged. I will not lose heart! The Lord will renew me. He will!" God wants to wipe away the negative and bring in the positive. He wants to give you new life in him. You don't have to be beaten down, because he carries you through.

Father, thank you for renewing me and for creating a fresh spirit within me. I will not lose heart, because I have you by my side. You are so good to me.

FACING THE SUN

If we say that we have fellowship with Him and yet walk in the darkness, we lie and do not practice the truth; but if we walk in the Light as He Himself is in the Light, we have fellowship with one another, and the blood of Jesus His Son cleanses us from all sin.

1 John 1:6-7 NASB

When we accept Christ as our Savior, our world suddenly brightens. It's as if things that were in shadows have quickly come into the sun. Walking in that light takes continued effort. It means making a daily commitment to follow the example Christ has set for us—doing what's right and rejecting what's wrong. Choosing to make the same decisions we made before our life with God means we are choosing darkness. Choosing to make decisions according to his Word means we are choosing life.

Doesn't it feel great when the sun shines on your face? Use that as a reminder to turn your face to the one who is light. Walk with God each day of your life, staying close to him. If you choose him, you choose life.

Lord, thank you for shining your light upon me. Help me turn away from the darkness in my life.

TROUBLE

*"I have told you these things, so that in me you
may have peace. In this world you will have trouble.
But take heart! I have overcome the world."*
JOHN 16:33 NIV

Some Christians believe that once they accept Christ
as their Savior, life will become much easier. *Presto! Poof!*
Like magic, pain and heartache will disappear and troubles
will stop. But that simply isn't true. The world we live in is
imperfect. Sad things and bad things will always be around.

That doesn't mean that there is no hope! Jesus is bigger
than the world we live in. He has overcome it! Someday
we'll live with him in a perfect place called heaven. But even
now we can have joy regardless of what's going on around
us. We can have peace because our hope doesn't depend
on circumstances; it depends on him.

*Lord, thank you for being my overcomer. Help me see past
the troubles around me and feel your joy instead.*

FEBRUARY

We are not saying that we can
do this work ourselves.
It is God who makes us able to do
all that we do.

2 Corinthians 3:5 NCV

HE HEARS

I love the LORD, because He has heard
My voice and my supplications.
Because He has inclined His ear to me,
Therefore I will call upon Him as long as I live.
PSALM 116:1-2 NKJV

Who's the first person you call when you need help? Do you shoot off a quick text to a friend? Call your mom? We usually turn to the people we know and trust. It's good to allow others in and to look to them for advice. But our first call, every time, should be to the Lord.

God always has a willing ear, and your calls always go through to him. He's eager to hear what you have to say. He's ready to listen—to be your first line of support. He isn't a far-off unapproachable God in the sky. He is available anytime and anywhere.

Father, thank you for hearing me when I need help. I'm so thankful you are always willing to be there for me and to love me.

WORRY-FREE

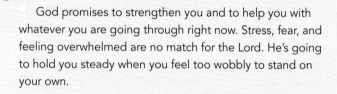

"Do not fear, for I am with you;
do not be dismayed, for I am your God.
I will strengthen you and help you;
I will uphold you with my righteous right hand."
Isaiah 41:10 NIV

God promises to strengthen you and to help you with whatever you are going through right now. Stress, fear, and feeling overwhelmed are no match for the Lord. He's going to hold you steady when you feel too wobbly to stand on your own.

God is with you. He is your God, and he is good. He never intended for you to live weighed down with worry. Instead, he'd love for you to throw all your cares on him. God is strong enough to take care of them. He's big enough to handle whatever you're willing to give him. You just have to allow him to help you.

Lord, thank you for strengthening me. I know that I do not have to fear because you are there for me.

JOY IN OBEDIENCE

This is the love of God, that we keep his commandments.
And his commandments are not burdensome.

1 JOHN 5:3 ESV

Loving God means keeping his commandments. That doesn't mean you're saved because of what you do. No, you're saved by grace. Still, the works you do and choices you make are going to be an extension of who you are—a child of God. As his child, you'll want to follow him and the example he sets. You'll willingly choose to live by his instructions.

If you have a close relationship with God, his commandments won't seem like a burden. As you follow him, you'll be tempted less and less to do what *you* want. Instead you'll start wanting what *he* wants. Following his commands will become a joy.

Father, thank you for giving me your commandments. I want to enjoy following them.

CHOOSING PEACE

Work at living in peace with everyone, and work at living a holy life, for those who are not holy will not see the Lord.
HEBREWS 12:14 NLT

Some people are easy to get along with. Others are just plain annoying. They smack their gum or talk nonstop or slurp their food. It takes everything you've got be kind to them. The Bible tells us that we have to work hard to get along with everybody. If fact, it says that if we don't work at it, we won't get a glimpse of the Lord in eternity. That's a pretty big statement!

Living in peace with those around us isn't something that comes naturally. That's why we need to pray that God will give us supernatural ability to do it. When we ask for his help, he is more than willing to give us what we need.

Father, thank you for helping me choose peace with the people in my life.

ULTIMATE GPS

My eyes are ever on the LORD,
for only he will release my feet from the snare.
PSALM 25:15

It's common sense to watch where you're going or you'll get tripped up. When it comes to walking with God, though, it's a different story. Instead of looking ahead and watching your every move, the Bible says to look directly at the Lord, every moment of your life. He'll keep you from whatever traps you may fall into.

Spend less time looking at the details of your life and more time with your eyes fixed on God. He is the ultimate GPS, and he will lead you exactly where you need to go. It's only when you take your eyes off him, that you'll fall right smack into the trap that the enemy sets for you. Stay close to God for direction.

Lord, thank you for directing me where to go and what steps to take. I pray that my eyes will always be on you.

TASTE AND SEE

O taste and see that the LORD is good;
How blessed is the man who takes refuge in Him!
PSALM 34:8 NASB

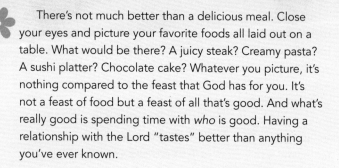

There's not much better than a delicious meal. Close your eyes and picture your favorite foods all laid out on a table. What would be there? A juicy steak? Creamy pasta? A sushi platter? Chocolate cake? Whatever you picture, it's nothing compared to the feast that God has for you. It's not a feast of food but a feast of all that's good. And what's really good is spending time with *who* is good. Having a relationship with the Lord "tastes" better than anything you've ever known.

The best part is that you can indulge in spending time with God whenever you want, day or night. Taste and see that the Lord is good. He's the best, and he wants to share with you all that he is and all that he has for you. He is so generous that way.

Lord, I want to taste all the good that you desire for me,
desiring you above all else, and taking refuge in your love.

REWARD OF HOPE

Lead me in your truth, and teach me,
for you are the God of my salvation;
for you I wait all day long.

PSALM 25:5 NRSV

When you are at your wit's end, who do you look to for help? If you are putting your hope in God, then you will never be let down. Hang on to his truth, allow him to teach you, and you'll find it's easier to hope.

Jesus died for you to be set free. He lives inside you and fills you with hope—because he is hope! He gives you hope for a future. There is no need to stumble, because he is for you. If that doesn't give you hope for what's to come, then nothing will. Put all your hope in him, and you will definitely see a reward.

Lord, I'm putting my hope and trust in you. Guide me in your truth. Teach me your ways. You are my Savior, and I'm so thankful for it!

ALL GOOD THINGS

Praise the LORD, my soul, and forget not all his benefits—
who forgives all your sins and heals all your diseases,
who redeems your life from the pit and
crowns you with love and compassion,
who satisfies your desires with good things so
that your youth is renewed like the eagle's.

PSALM 103:2-5 NIV

Everything we have is a gift from the Lord. Forgiveness, mercy, health, and all good things come from him. We would be nowhere without him. If it weren't for him, we'd have to face eternity without any hope.

Because of his kindness, God decided instead to "crown us with love and compassion." That doesn't mean that only good things will happen. But it does mean that God is faithful and promises to be with us always. Nothing can separate us from his love. He has saved our lives and wrapped us in his goodness.

Father, thank you for your forgiving heart. I give you all
praise, because all good things come from you.

WEIGHT LIFTED

*"I will forgive them for the wicked things they did,
and I will not remember their sins anymore."*

HEBREWS 8:12 NCV

When someone has done us wrong, it's hard to forgive much less forget. We've got long memories when it comes to the injustices we see in our lives. Thank goodness that's not how the Lord operates! He loves and forgives us. When we confess we're wrong, he forgives us and makes is as though we'd never sinned at all. Everything is wiped clean. He doesn't hold onto the list of our failings for future reference.

Knowing that gives us freedom. We don't have to be weighed down under guilt from the past. It's as if God has taken a huge weight that was pressing down upon us, and lifted it right off. There is no need to punish ourselves over and over. He's forgiven and forgotten.

Lord, thank you for forgiving my sins. I praise you even more for forgetting them entirely, wiping them from my history. I am constantly amazed by who you are.

HELD TOGETHER

He is before all things, and in Him all things consist.
COLOSSIANS 1:17 NKJV

Jesus is the glue that holds all things together. He was in existence before anything else was. Everything—the heavens, the earth, and everything in them—was made by him. He always was and always will be.

Let that soak in for a moment. If he can hold the world together, he can hold you, no matter what is happening. When things seem like they're falling apart, he wants you to go to him. Let Jesus pick up the pieces and hold you in the palm of his hand.

Lord, thank you for being the one who holds me together. I'm so thankful for your sacrifice. Thank you for rescuing me. I pray I'd look to you when I feel like I'm falling apart.

PREOCCUPIED

Set your minds on things above, not on earthly things.

COLOSSIANS 3:2 NIV

Clothes, school, cell phones, music, homework. It's seems impossible not to think about all these things. Yet God tells us to set our mind on things above, to turn our thoughts toward him and heaven. We're surrounded by messages all day that tell us what to wear, how to look, and what latest thing we need in our lives. Those things aren't necessarily bad, but when our minds become so preoccupied with them that they become our focus, it's time to make a change.

God wants us to enjoy what we've been given, yet not grasp them so firmly that we're unwilling to part with them. That's because he knows the best is yet to come. Our true priorities should be on the things that last.

Lord, help me to put my mind where it should be. Open my eyes to see your everlasting kingdom.

WISDOM IN WAITING

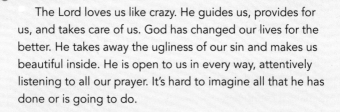

Everything is appropriate in its own time. But though God has planted eternity in the hearts of men, even so, many cannot see the whole scope of God's work from beginning to end.

ECCLESIASTES 3:11 TLB

The Lord loves us like crazy. He guides us, provides for us, and takes care of us. God has changed our lives for the better. He takes away the ugliness of our sin and makes us beautiful inside. He is open to us in every way, attentively listening to all our prayer. It's hard to imagine all that he has done or is going to do.

Sometimes, though, it seems like we have to wait forever for his answers. We want to know everything he has planned right this moment, but it's just not meant to be. Through waiting, we can learn patience, humility, and so much more. Being made to wait doesn't reflect a lack of interest or love on God's part. Rather, it's his infinite wisdom that keeps us close to him, learning to trust him even though not everything is clear.

Father, thank you that there's wisdom to be found in the waiting.

BETTER WAYS

"My thoughts are nothing like your thoughts," says the LORD. "And my ways are far beyond anything you could imagine."
ISAIAH 55:8 NLT

How many times has your life taken a turn in a direction you just didn't like? "God, what are you thinking?" you might say. "How can this be your plan?" Sometimes we try to work out things logically, based on what we know. Yet the Lord tells us that he doesn't think like we do. He's got a bigger picture in mind. God knows what's best, even when his best isn't at all obvious.

It's hard to trust his will when the end of the path isn't clear. It can be incredibly difficult to be patient and push through tough times. But God is wise, and he knows everything. His thoughts are not like ours, and that's a good thing! We can trust in his plan, his timing, and his goodness.

Lord, I know your ways are better than mine. Help me to trust in your plan.

THE SMOOTH WAY

*You provide a broad path for my feet,
so that my ankles do not give way.*

2 Samuel 22:37 NIV

If you've ever sprained an ankle, you know the tendons and ligaments inside stretch in an abnormal way. That can leave someone susceptible to reinjuring the same ankle again, simply because it's been pushed in a way that it shouldn't have been. It's the same with sin. Once you give in, the tendency is to make the same mistake again. It's as if the "muscle memory" has been pulled the wrong way, and you remember exactly what to do to head in the wrong direction.

The Lord is faithful to provide a way out. God creates a path that is smooth and good for walking. If you listen to his voice and do what he says, your ankles won't give out; you won't slip into sin again.

Father, thank you for giving me a broad path on which to walk. I pray that I would always choose to follow your way instead of my own.

YOU ARE STRONG

*It is God who arms me with strength
and keeps my way secure.*
PSALM 18:32 NIV

No matter how big or small you are, you are a force to be reckoned with. That's because your strength comes from more than just your muscles. Your might comes from a place that is more powerful than any other on earth—God. He gives you strength and encouragement even when you feel it's hard to press through.

Keep your chin up, no matter what you're going through. You are strong. You've got God behind you. When you begin to doubt, just know that the Lord is right there, ready to fight for and with you. He believes that you are worth the fight!

Lord, I'm humbled by your willingness to stand with me. Thank you for giving me your strength when I don't have any of my own.

FIRST RESPONSE

*When I was in trouble, I called to the Lord,
and he answered me.*

PSALM 120:1 NCV

When you are struggling, the first place you need to go is to the Lord. The biggest temptation is to turn to friends. Friends give you instant feedback, agree with you, and affirm you. But the Lord is ready with a better answer than anything your friends could give. If you call out to him, he will listen. When you cry for help, he is eager to give it.

So often, people make the mistake of picturing God as this mysterious person in the sky, someone aloof and distant. But he wants a relationship with you. He longs to hear your voice and spend time with you. When you take your troubles to him, he will answer your prayers! Just listen to his voice, and he'll answer.

Father, thank you for hearing my cries. I want you to be the first person I go to when I'm struggling.

JOY AND PEACE

*May the God of hope fill you with all joy and peace
as you trust in him, so that you may overflow
with hope by the power of the Holy Spirit.*

ROMANS 15:13 NIV

We tend to confuse joy with happiness. In fact, they're two very different things. Happiness is based on circumstances. When things get tough, happiness flees. Joy, though, isn't based on what's happening. It comes from knowing that God is in control. And peace? Peace is being restful when you are in the middle of a struggle.

If we pray for a spirit of joy and peace and put our hope in God, he promises us joy and peace. They come from his Spirit. The Lord wants to fill us up to the point of overflowing with his love. Out of that love comes true joy, peace, and hope!

Lord, I'm putting my trust in you today. Fill me with your joy.

DELIVERED FROM FEAR

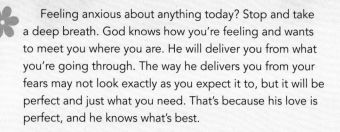

I sought the LORD, and He heard me,
And delivered me from all my fears.

PSALM 34:4 NKJV

Feeling anxious about anything today? Stop and take a deep breath. God knows how you're feeling and wants to meet you where you are. He will deliver you from what you're going through. The way he delivers you from your fears may not look exactly as you expect it to, but it will be perfect and just what you need. That's because his love is perfect, and he knows what's best.

When you feel like there is nowhere else to turn, know that you are never alone. The Lord loves you so much. He cares about the smallest details of your life, so think how much more he cares about big problems and anxieties. He will guide you through them all.

Father, I give you my fears. Please take them away. I'm seeking you and your presence today, knowing how much you love me.

GOD'S TOOLBOX

I have hidden your word in my heart
that I might not sin against you.
PSALM 119:11 NIV

Learning Scripture is one of the most powerful things you can do. Why? Turning it over and over in your mind will make different bits of wisdom come to the surface. You'll find something new to be learned, even from the same old passages. Best of all, learning God's Word is like tucking it away, so it's ready to pop out when you need it.

If someone asks you a question that requires discernment, God's truth will already be in you if you've taken the time to memorize it. When you are struggling, you'll easily be able to bring his words to mind. There are so many words of comfort in the Bible. When you are sad, you can turn to them. And your resistance to temptation is only strengthened when you have his wisdom deep inside your heart. The Bible is like God's toolbox, full of what you need to live out life.

Lord, thank you for giving me your truth. I will gladly hide your words in my heart.

TO-DO LISTS

*Now to Him who is able to do far more abundantly beyond
all that we ask or think, according to the power that
works within us, to Him be the glory in the church and in
Christ Jesus to all generations forever and ever. Amen.*
EPHESIANS 3:20-21 NASB

Imagine you've got a full day, packed with a long to-do
list. You cross one thing after another off your list, each time
satisfied that you've accomplished so much in such a short
time.

Now imagine God's to-do list. His list is so much longer
than our longest list, and yet he easily does it all. He is able
to accomplish so much more than we could ever ask him or
imagine. What's even more amazing is that he accomplishes
many things *through us*. When we serve him, we're allowing
him to use us for his kingdom. Isn't he incredible? He is
worthy of all our praise and deserves all the glory we can
give him.

*Lord, thank you for using me to spread your kingdom. I pray
for a willing heart.*

GLOWING

The law of the LORD is perfect, reviving the soul;
the decrees of the LORD are sure, making wise the simple;
the precepts of the LORD are right, rejoicing the heart;
the commandment of the LORD is
clear, enlightening the eyes.

PSALM 19:7-8 NRSV

Some people have something special about them. They almost glow from inside. That's the kind of beauty that following God's ways can give you. It's a beauty that can't be replicated or outdone by anything synthetic or put on.

The Bible tells that following the laws of God refreshes your soul. He can make you wise just by giving you the knowledge to do what's right. God gives you a lasting joy that surpasses any happiness. When you choose to walk with him, he makes you radiant. If you follow him every day, you'll stand out for your radiant spirit.

Father, I pray that I would follow you all the days of my life,
seeking your joy and love.

JOYFUL SONG

Make a joyful noise to the LORD, all the earth!
Serve the LORD with gladness!
Come into his presence with singing!
PSALM 100:1-2 ESV

Ever feel so happy you just want to sing? Singing is one of the ways we can express to God how much we love him. There's nothing like the joy that knowing the Lord brings us, and it only makes sense that his love would make us want to sing his praise. And we're encouraged to do just that!

Worshipping the Lord with song is a concept that has been around for ages. When we come before him with joyful songs, we are joining scores of believers from years past and all of heaven as well. Together we praise him. God loves to hear you sing. Praise him like he deserves to be praised.

Father, I'm full of praise for you, and I just want to sing.
I want to give you the worship you deserve.
I'm in awe of who you are.

MY SHIELD

LORD, you are my shield,
my wonderful God who gives me courage.
PSALM 3:3 NCV

In ancient battles, soldiers used a shield to protect themselves from the arrows shot against them. Placing that shield between them and the enemy was the one thing that saved them.

Sometimes in life it may feel like you're under attack. Gossip, cutting remarks, or being treated unfairly may be getting you down. The Lord is like a shield. He's your protector. All you need to do is call on him for help, and he'll be there. He'll help you hold your head up high even when you can't do it on your own.

Lord, thank you for the ways in which you protect me from the pain of this world.

A BEAUTIFUL PLAN

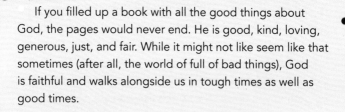

LORD, you are my God;
I will exalt you and praise your name,
for in perfect faithfulness
you have done wonderful things.

ISAIAH 25:1 NIV

If you filled up a book with all the good things about God, the pages would never end. He is good, kind, loving, generous, just, and fair. While it might not like seem like that sometimes (after all, the world of full of bad things), God is faithful and walks alongside us in tough times as well as good times.

He has a beautiful plan for your life. But he won't force that plan on you. Instead he loves you by giving you a choice—to follow his plan or leave it. He knows his plan is best. It bubbles up from a heart that loves you deeply and knows you intimately. Will you trust him?

Lord, thank you for knowing every detail of my life and
caring enough about me to plan each step.

BETTER THAN LIFE

Because your steadfast love is better than life,
my lips will praise you.
So I will bless you as long as I live;
I will lift up my hands and call on your name.

PSALM 63:3-4 NRSV

We have a tendency to cling pretty hard to the stuff in our lives—our home, our clothes, our shoes, our electronics, our music. Even our friends, our home, and family can seem to be the most important things of all. And yet, the Bible tells us that God's love is better than life. That love is better than anything or anyone we have or know.

When you spend time with God in prayer and reading his Word, you become even more aware of God's amazing love. Everything else pales in comparison. The more you know how much God loves you, the more you'll find that trusting and praising him comes naturally.

God, your love is breathtaking. I can't wrap my head around how much you love me.

BE STILL

"Be still, and know that I am God;
I will be exalted among the nations,
I will be exalted in the earth."
PSALM 46:10 NIV

Satan is a powerful opponent of ours. He tries to feed us lies, whispering in different ways that God is bad and that sin is best. That we aren't good enough. That we are failures. And the list goes on and on.

If you ever find that happening, take a deep breath and be still. Remember that God is far more powerful than the enemy. He is God! The enemy doesn't stand a chance. Then remember that God loves you very much. Breathe deep, be still, and soak up the truth of God's love.

Father, I give you all the praise today. Help me to block out the whispers of the enemy, and be still in the knowledge that you are God.

GIFT OF MUSIC

*Let the word of Christ dwell in you richly, teaching
and admonishing one another in all wisdom,
singing psalms and hymns and spiritual songs,
with thankfulness in your hearts to God.*

COLOSSIANS 3:16 ESV

Every small detail of your life should be done in the
name of Christ Jesus. You can praise him with every fiber of
your being. You can be thankful to him for the richness of
all the blessings he gives. When you hear his Word, you can
soak it in and let it take over. You'll be rewarded for doing
so, since you'll experience life in fuller way.

One of the ways God gives us to praise and thank him
is through psalms, hymns, and worship songs. Music is also
a great way to learn Scripture. Putting melody to a verse is
one of the best ways to memorize it. Through music we lift
God up and celebrate who he is and what he's done.

*Lord, thank you for the gift of music. I want to sing your
praises all day long, telling others of your great goodness.*

A GIFT TO BE GIVEN

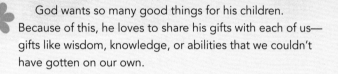

Earnestly desire the greater gifts.
And I show you a still more excellent way.

1 CORINTHIANS 12:31 NASB

God wants so many good things for his children. Because of this, he loves to share his gifts with each of us— gifts like wisdom, knowledge, or abilities that we couldn't have gotten on our own.

God is free with his gifts, but here's the funny thing about them: they're not for us to keep. We're supposed to share them with others. When God's love inside us starts to grow, we suddenly want to give the gift of discernment, hospitality, generosity, and more to others. God gives us gifts so we can give, encouraging and blessing those around us. How can you use your gifts to bless someone else?

Lord, your gifts are better than anything else I could receive. Thank you for allowing me to be a blessing to others.

MARCH

He has granted to us his precious and
very great promises, so that through
them you may become partakers
of the divine nature,
having escaped from the corruption
that is in the world.

2 PETER 1:3-4 ESV

DON'T GIVE UP

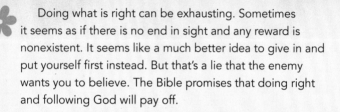

Let us not become weary in doing good, for at the proper time we will reap a harvest if we do not give up.
GALATIANS 6:9 NIV

Doing what is right can be exhausting. Sometimes it seems as if there is no end in sight and any reward is nonexistent. It seems like a much better idea to give in and put yourself first instead. But that's a lie that the enemy wants you to believe. The Bible promises that doing right and following God will pay off.

If you plant a field, you have to be patient for the harvest to come at the right time. Pick your crop too early, and it won't be ripe. Too late, and it'll be rotten. God's timing is perfect. He wants the best for you and will give you a full harvest if you continue to work patiently. Just don't give up!

Lord, show me your timing and continue to give me strength to do what's right.

ALWAYS WELCOME

If we confess our sins, he will forgive our sins,
because we can trust God to do what is right. He will
cleanse us from all the wrongs we have done.

1 JOHN 1:9 NCV

God tells us again and again that if we confess our sin, forgiveness is ours. Sometimes shame, pride, and even fear hold us back from coming to the Lord and asking for what he has already promised. We stand at the doorway of his home, not sure if we are welcome.

But we are always welcome! We never have to give in to hesitation or embarrassment or be afraid of his response. God is everything a good father is. He is kind, forgiving, and gentle. He won't refuse our request for forgiveness, because there's nothing more he'd like than to have a close relationship with us.

Jesus, when my fear or my pride stops me from coming
to you, draw me in with your kindness. Thanks for never
turning me away. Thank you for washing me clean and
making me new again.

TRUE CONTENTMENT

*Keep your lives free from the love of money
and be content with what you have.*

HEBREWS 13:5 NIV

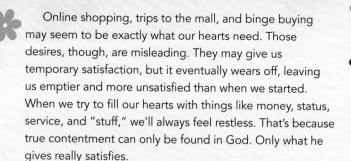

Online shopping, trips to the mall, and binge buying may seem to be exactly what our hearts need. Those desires, though, are misleading. They may give us temporary satisfaction, but it eventually wears off, leaving us emptier and more unsatisfied than when we started. When we try to fill our hearts with things like money, status, service, and "stuff," we'll always feel restless. That's because true contentment can only be found in God. Only what he gives really satisfies.

One of the things he gives is the gift of each day. Every day in itself is a gift from God. Focusing on today and what God has for us in it—not on what happened yesterday or what will happen tomorrow—keeps us present. He wants us to take hold of today, without wondering what is next or if there is more.

Jesus, quiet my heart when it's restless. Open my eyes to the blessings that I'll find in simple moments. Make me grow more content as you open up my eyes to the wonderful day you have given me.

A GOOD FRIENDSHIP

Do not be deceived: "Bad company ruins good morals."
1 CORINTHIANS 15:33 ESV

Ever walked away from a friend feeling sad and heavy? Relationships can either lift you up or tear you down. Be careful of close friendships that only speak negativity and destruction into your life, especially if those friends encourage you to compromise your morals or do something against your values. If you start compromising your faith to appease a friendship, that should be a warning that the friend may not be a good friend after all. Maybe a little distance would be helpful.

Good and true friends encourage you to do what is right—all the time. If you surround yourself with friends that have their eyes on Jesus, who encourage you, and speak life and truth, you'll be a stronger person. Jesus' design was that friendships would better you, not tear you down.

Jesus, please help me to sift through any negative influences in my life. Thank you for the gift of good friends. Thank you for friends who bring light to my life and who have good intentions. Thank you for friends that inspire me to live a life for you, and only you.

ANGER UNDER CONTROL

Be humble and gentle. Be patient with each other, making allowance for each other's faults because of your love.

EPHESIANS 4:2 TLB

When we're hot with anger, disappointment, and frustration, initially it might feel good to release our temper without restraint or a second thought. It's easy to feel justified with an angry reaction. But soon after we erupt, that good feeling doesn't feel so good. It's quickly replaced with regret and sometimes shame. Our anger can hurt us and the people we love.

We all feel anger from time to time; it's a normal and common emotion. But our anger doesn't have to control us. In those moments we have the God-given ability to resist our feelings of irritation and choose patience instead, ultimately choosing to love. Learning to take a deep breath, whispering a prayer, and meditating on Scripture are all ways that help us keep from giving in to anger. Focusing on God's goodness and grace makes letting go of anger much easier.

Jesus, fill me with your love for others. Teach me your patience and grace. I want to be quick to offer forgiveness, instead of quick to let my temper control my reactions.

BOLDNESS

*We say with confidence, "The LORD is
my helper; I will not be afraid."*
PSALM 118:6 NIV

When we picture someone who is bold, we tend to think
of someone who is big, mighty, and strong. Because many
of us don't fit that description, we don't think of ourselves as
bold. We look at our own size, strength, and limitations, and
determine that we don't have the kind of courage needed
to face a situation. Too many times we let self-doubt inhibit
our true abilities.

God didn't give us a spirit of fear. Recognizing that God
is our helper breathes boldness into us. It is because of him
that we can be bold, confident, and strong in whatever is
ahead. Our strength, status, and size don't determine how
bold we can be, God does. Knowing he is our help makes
us stand up with courage and boldness.

*God, thank you that I don't have to live in fear. I can live in
boldness and confidence instead. I am grateful that you are
my strong helper and you never leave my side.*

INFLUENCING VOICES

Brothers and sisters, think about the things that are good and worthy of praise. Think about the things that are true and honorable and right and pure and beautiful and respected. Do what you learned and received from me, what I told you, and what you saw me do. And the God who gives peace will be with you.

PHILIPPIANS 4:8-9 NCV

There are many influences in this world, each one speaking to us in different ways. Sorting out which voices are good and bad can be confusing. From time to time, it's helpful to pause and take a minute to ask, "What voice am I allowing to influence my life, my heart, and my mind?" Words are powerful. They can breathe life. Or they can cause death.

The verse above is the perfect guide for deciding what helpful and what's not. If something is true and noble and right, that voice will point us to Jesus and encourage us to live a life for him. If it's something lovely or excellent or praiseworthy, that influence will draw us close to God. Anything that doesn't fit in this category will pull us away from what is him.

Jesus, of all the voices in the world, I want to hear yours the clearest. Help me to grow to recognize your voice and know it well. Help me to think what's true and lovely and good. I want to follow it all the days of my life.

CREATIVE SKILLS

He has filled him with the Spirit of God, with wisdom, with understanding, with knowledge and with all kinds of skills— to make artistic designs for work in gold, silver and bronze.
EXODUS 35:31-32 NLT

We see God's creativity around us in the unending sky, the deep blue oceans, the lush rainforests, and majestic mountaintops. We see his imagination in the creatures of the sea and in the variety of wildlife. As a master at his craft, God made us in his image. We are his best masterpieces. From our eye color to our personality, God designed everything with care and skill.

His creativity is everywhere—including inside you and me. God is creative, and he made us to be creative too. We all have different sets of talents and abilities that come from God. He loves the creative side of us, so we shouldn't stifle it, but embrace it. When we use our creative talent, we can use it with a heart of gratitude, good stewardship, and confidence.

God, your creativity brings me so much joy. Thank you for creating me in your image and giving me talents and abilities. Help me use those gifts today and every day for your glory.

A GOD OF MIRACLES

*"Did I not tell you that if you believed,
you would see the glory of God?"*
JOHN 11:40 NRSV

God is a God of miracles. He loves to show up in
big ways in our lives. Faith in God is believing, without
hesitation, that he is in the midst of every part of our lives.
Sometimes our lack of faith blinds us to the glory of God.
We miss out on witnessing miracles simply because our
faith is weak. We can't see his glory because our hearts are
completely shut off toward it, or maybe because of doubt,
pessimism, or cynicism. We spend our energy doubting
instead of believing.

When we have faith, we look for God's presence in our
lives, trusting that every day brings evidence of him. When
we believe in God, we can expect to see him working and
doing great things.

*Jesus, I know that every day you are at work in my life in
huge ways. Help me silence voices of doubt, pessimism,
and cynicism and open my eyes to your glory. I long to see
you written all over my life story.*

CREATED BY LOVE

God is love.
1 JOHN 4:8 NLT

We all have those days where we don't feel loved, understood, noticed, or appreciated. Those days are difficult, and we can feel incredibly sad and lonely. Sometimes those days stretch to longer periods, and we might start buying into the idea that we don't matter. That cycle of depression is heartbreaking and debilitating.

The reality is that God sees you, understands you, appreciates you, and loves you—immensely. When others might call you worthless, he calls you valuable, prized, and treasured. He loves you so much that he gave his life for you. When you feel your self-worth threatened, remember you were created by a God of love. You are loved.

God, your love encourages me. When I feel unloved by the world, you remind me so gently just how much you love and care for me. Thank you.

TOTAL DEPENDENCE

> *"If you sinful people know how to give good gifts to your children, how much more will your heavenly Father give good gifts to those who ask him."*
>
> MATTHEW 7:11 NLT

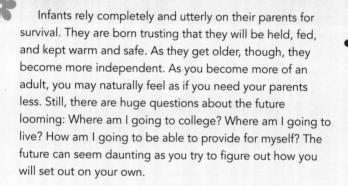

Infants rely completely and utterly on their parents for survival. They are born trusting that they will be held, fed, and kept warm and safe. As they get older, though, they become more independent. As you become more of an adult, you may naturally feel as if you need your parents less. Still, there are huge questions about the future looming: Where am I going to college? Where am I going to live? How am I going to be able to provide for myself? The future can seem daunting as you try to figure out how you will set out on your own.

Even though you outgrow your need for complete dependence on a parent, you never outgrow your need for God. You don't have to have all the answers to your future. You can take comfort in knowing that God is a faithful God, he loves you, and he will provide for every need.

Jesus, as I get older, I pray I'd never grow away from you. I don't want to fear the future but trust in your tender care. May I depend on you for everything I need.

NEED FOR FRIENDS

As for me, how good it is to be near God!
PSALM 73:28 NLT

Deep down inside many people are afraid of being alone. For them, the thought of walking through life without a friend to share struggles and happiness with is a crushing thought. We were designed to live in friendship with others. When we don't have that kind of community, the temptation is to fill up that need with other things like shopping, eating, exercise, or entertainment. But they're no substitute for a good friend that stands by your side.

God knows our need for friends, so we can come to him and ask him for that exactly—a good friend we can talk, laugh, and cry with. What God really longs for is for us to be near him and to know him. He wants us to know we will never be completely alone. He is the best friend of all who can heal the ache in our hearts.

Jesus, fill the loneliness in me with your presence. When I feel empty, make me aware of your faithful friendship. Your friendship is a comfort in a sometimes lonely world.

SOURCE OF CONFIDENCE

Truly he is my rock and my salvation;
he is my fortress, I will never be shaken.
PSALM 62:2 NIV

What makes you feel confident? New lip gloss? Trendy clothes? Great grades? All these are good things that can boost your self-esteem, but ask yourself, "What is it that allows me to stand straight, hold my head high, and face challenges head on?" The one thing that will keep your identity from being derailed is knowing that your value comes from God.

When it comes from the world and material objects, confidence is easily shaken. It can be shaken by careless and hurtful words from others. It can be shaken by a bad grade, a missed opportunity, or comparing yourself with others. But if God is the source of your confidence, you can take your cues from him. He will build you up with his truth, love, and encouragement. Insecurities and doubts will be silenced quickly with his affirmation.

Lord, sometimes I struggle with feeling confident. Remind
me that my confidence comes from you.

STANDARD OF PERFECTION

*Let us then approach God's throne of grace with
confidence, so that we may receive mercy and
find grace to help us in our time of need.*

HEBREWS 4:16 NIV

I messed up again. I can never get it right. Do these
thoughts sound familiar? Sometimes the cruelest statements
come from within us. They can be some of the most
dangerous. Because we are human, we are bound to make
mistakes, but that doesn't mean we should beat ourselves up.

Striving for perfection will only bring us down again
and again. It is impossible and discouraging to live up to a
standard of perfection. Instead we can be kind to ourselves
just like God is kind to us. God views us with grace. When
we do mess up, we can come to God, knowing he'll
welcome us and pour his grace and love over us. He knows
our hearts, and he forgives, readily and eagerly.

*God, help me to see myself as you see me. Thank you for
your unending kindness and grace. I am so grateful that you
love me despite all of my mistakes.*

SLAVE TO TEMPTATION

The temptations in your life are no different from what others experience. And God is faithful. He will not allow the temptation to be more than you can stand. When you are tempted, he will show you a way out so that you can endure.

1 CORINTHIANS 10:13 NLT

Do you ever feel like you are a slave to your temptations and weaknesses? Temptation is common, and sometimes it can feel utterly defeating. You feel weak and hopeless. In the middle of a struggle, you might look at people around you and wonder how they seem to have it all together. *Why am I always struggling, but they aren't?*

The truth is that everyone struggles. Fighting temptation is a battle for every Christian. Just because we are battling, though, it doesn't mean we are failing. As God's children we don't have to be slaves to our desires. He gives us power to be victorious in every weaknesses and temptation. We can be victorious because God declares us so. Even in our weakest moments, we know that God will provide a way out.

God, sometimes I get tired struggling with temptation. I feel weak and sometimes my desires threaten to overtake me. Thank you, Lord, that you always make a way for me to have victory. Show me that way out, Lord. Keep me close to you.

COURAGE TO STAND

"Have I not commanded you? Be strong and courageous.
Do not be afraid; do not be discouraged, for the
LORD your God will be with you wherever you go."

JOSHUA 1:9 NASB

It takes courage to stand up for what is right. Following God won't necessarily make you popular. In fact, sometimes following God means that you won't be liked for your choices, values, and opinions. Many times, being a Christian makes you a red fish in a big pond of blue fishes. Being that red fish takes courage.

It can be hard to stand out and even harder to feel ridiculed for our choices. In some ways it would be easier to stay silent, avoiding judgment. Our need to be accepted is strong. Yet God applauds our courage. He knows the difficulties we face every day, and he wants us to know that we aren't alone. He is with us. Every courageous step we take, we take with him.

Jesus, I want to live my life for you. Sometimes I'm afraid of standing out and being made fun of or rejected. Give me courage, God, when I want to hide my faith and simply blend in. Thank you that I'm never alone.

NOT DEFINED

It is for freedom that Christ has set us free.
Stand firm, then, and do not let yourselves be
burdened again by a yoke of slavery.

GALATIANS 5:1 NIV

Too often we let our past define us. We may be ashamed of choices we made or the life we lived before following God. The things that used to be can blur the new life we have.

You aren't defined by your past. Whoever you were or whatever you did before God gave you a new life is irrelevant. God gave you freedom. He gave you a new identity. So when you tell your story, you can say with confidence, "I was saved by grace." God is the light in all your stories, even the darkest ones. His grace and name redefine you. Take hold of the freedom he wants you to have.

God, I am so humbled that you've freed me from my past.
Thank you that I'm not defined by what I was. Help me
embrace the new identity you've given me.

NOT HOPELESS

All that the Father gives me will come to me, and
whoever comes to me I will never cast out.

JOHN 6:37 ESV

Do you know how much God really loves us? He knows our weaknesses and struggles, and he loves us deeply despite them. When we feel unlovable and unworthy, it can stop us from seeking God. We often feel undeserving of his love and care. We look at ourselves and refuse to believe that God could possibly welcome us. So instead of walking toward him, where we belong, we walk away.

But God does welcome us. Not only does he welcome us, but he seeks us out. He even goes after those who the world defines as hopeless and unworthy. There is nothing that we can do that will stop God from loving us. When all we can see is failure, he sees beauty. He wants to redeem our lives and make us his. He loves us for who we are.

God, thank you for accepting me. I don't feel worthy of your love or warm embrace, but I am so thankful for them. Thank you for your redemption in my life.

REST AND RELAXATION

*"Come to me, all you who are weary and
burdened, and I will give you rest."*
MATTHEW 11:28 NIV

When we hear the word *relaxation*, we usually think of vacation: sunshine, sandy beaches, lazing by the ocean, and soaking up some much needed rest. But those types of vacation are few and far between and for many people nonexistent.

A vacation or a break from life may not be a possibility, but that doesn't mean rest can't, and shouldn't, happen. It's easy to get caught up in thinking that being busy means we are super important. It is good to have goals—God created us to work hard—but rest is also needed. It isn't a luxury but a necessity, and it's vital for our soul's health. For some of us, we need to make a priority every day of letting go of our stress and worries and meditating on God's Word.

Jesus wants us to be our place of rest and restoration. When life gets too chaotic and crazy, he wants us to spend time with him. In that place of rest, he'll give us new hope and strength.

God, thank you for rest and for creating my body to crave rest. In you I find rest from the busyness and trouble around me. Thank you for renewing my heart when I choose to get away and spend time with you.

STAYING PURE

Run from sexual sin! No other sin so clearly affects the body as this one does. For sexual immorality is a sin against your own body. Don't you realize that your body is the temple of the Holy Spirit, who lives in you and was given to you by God? You do not belong to yourself, for God bought you with a high price. So you must honor God with your body.

1 CORINTHIANS 6:18-20 NLT

Sex. You see it glorified everywhere—on TV, in music lyrics, on billboards. The message is that sexuality is something to put on display. By staying pure, you are led to think you are missing out on the most exciting thing ever. The truth is that your sexuality is something to be protected, honored, and saved for the right time and the right person.

Sex is amazing, but it was created for marriage. Outside of marriage, sex leaves you unguarded and vulnerable. God doesn't want you to wait to have sex because he wants to deny you fun and pleasure. Rather, he wants you to wait because he knows how painful an intimate experience can be at the wrong time. He wants to protect you from unnecessary harm. He has your heart in mind when he says, "Wait."

God, sex is a gift worth waiting for. Help me to stay pure in a world that encourages sexual relationships outside of your perfect plan. Give me patience to wait and strength to protect my purity.

NO ROOM FOR FEAR

*There is no fear in love; but perfect love casts
out fear, because fear involves punishment, and
the one who fears is not perfected in love.*

1 JOHN 4:18 NASB

Fear is an unkind ruler who dictates your choices and
your attitude. Fear is a liar who unfairly toys with your
emotions and persuades you to doubt. Fear is a distraction
that pulls you away from God's calling on your life. Fear is a
manipulator who twists your view of God and your hope for
the future. Fear is a killer who attacks the joy in your life and
replaces it with anxiety.

God's love is a weapon against fear. Fear doesn't have
to rule us because God is a God of truth, peace, kindness,
life, and love. Knowing we're loved by God means we don't
have to give fear a place. God will drive out the fear that
taunts us and quiet our anxious minds with his peace.

*Jesus, when fear grips me, remind me that your love grips
my heart tighter. Thank you for driving away my anxious
thoughts. Thank you for giving me a life of peace where fear
doesn't have room to make its home.*

EMBRACE THE DAY

*The LORD is my strength and my defense;
he has become my salvation.
He is my God, and I will praise him,
my father's God, and I will exalt him.*

EXODUS 15:2 NIV

How we start our day can make all the difference in our attitude and outlook on life. A healthy breakfast, some exercise, and a relaxing routine are great ways to start, but what do our souls need? Rolling out of bed, we can grumble about having to finish a homework assignment, complain that we have to spend the day at school, or get upset that we have to watch our sibling. Or, we can choose to wake with praise and gratitude for a new day. We can choose to start the day with thankfulness.

We have so much to be thankful for, and that thanks is due to God. Recognizing that every day is a gift gives us a fresh perspective. Instead of dreading the day ahead, we can embrace it with hope and joy.

God, regardless of what is going on, teach me to stop, look up, and praise you for your goodness in my life. I am so thankful and humbled by your everyday blessings.

RELEASING WORRY

"Don't worry about these things, saying, 'What will we eat? What will we drink? What will we wear?' These things dominate the thoughts of unbelievers, but your heavenly Father already knows all your needs."

MATTHEW 6:31-32 NLT

Worry is a heavy burden to carry. Worry can cause us to lose hope. It damages our spirits and our spiritual, mental, and emotional health. The more we worry, the more it can grow and affect all our relationships, including our relationship with the Lord. It is a burden that the Lord doesn't want us to own, which is why he tells us again and again to bring all our worries to him.

Why continue to wrestle with worry when we don't have to? We don't have to exhaust our hearts and spirits. Trusting God is the answer to getting rid of anxiety. He is the only answer for complete freedom and peace. When we feel anxious, we can go to the Lord and he promises to fill us with peace and understanding.

Lord, you tell me to release all of my cares and burdens to you. Thank you that you guard my spirit, heart, and mind from worry. I'm grateful that I can cling to your promises. I trust you.

MISPLACED WORDS

A perverse person stirs up conflict, and
a gossip separates close friends.
PROVERBS 16:28 NIV

If you've been on the receiving end of gossip, you know how much power words have. Learning that people you thought were your friends are whispering behind your back can be painful. Hurtful and misplaced words can break your heart and spirit.

We all love to talk and share what's on our hearts, but there is a point when talking and sharing can be destructive. That's especially true if our stories are twisted and exaggerated for shock value or entertainment. If what we are saying isn't loving, true, and glorifying to God, we should be changing the topic of conversation. Our words can give life to another person or they can do some serious damage. If we love well, we'll take great care to talk with our friends about things that are positive, true, and encouraging.

Jesus, forgive me if my conversations have caused others hurt and heartache. Use my words to lift up and encourage those around me.

STANDING STRONG

Stand firm then, with the belt of truth buckled around your waist, with the breastplate of righteousness in place, and with your feet fitted with the readiness that comes from the gospel of peace. In addition to all this, take up the shield of faith, with which you can extinguish all the flaming arrows of the evil one. Take the helmet of salvation and the sword of the Spirit, which is the word of God.

EPHESIANS 6:14-17 NIV

In times of trouble, sometimes we feel like we can't stand strong. We panic and feel incapable and unprotected. However, God never leaves us unguarded and unequipped. He has given us weapons for our protection, to be ready for whatever battle we have. He gave us truth, righteousness, peace, faith, salvation, and the Word of God. But what good are weapons if they sit there dusty, untouched, and unused?

Pick your weapons up and use them. When you're going through a hard time, remember what's true and remember that God has forgiven you and given you a new life of righteousness. Claim the peace that he promises. Pick up the shield of faith and say, "God, I believe in you. I trust you to take care of me and show me what to do." Then read God's Word and focus on its truth.

Lord, I am so grateful for the weapons you have given me for my protection. Thank you that you've equipped me for every battle I face. Thank you for your unending protection.

HOPE WITHIN REACH

*What we suffer now is nothing compared
to the glory he will reveal to us later.*
ROMANS 8:18 NLT

When we're suffering, it is hard to believe that there's going to be an end to it. Sometimes the pain is so great, that it's hard to focus on anything else. Suffering often keeps us from seeing outside our current situation. Our perspective is shortened, and all of our senses are focused on what's happening right now.

God promises that joy will come. That joy will completely overwhelm any suffering we've had; there won't be any comparison. The pain and the heartache we feel on this earth is only temporary; it is not eternal. So in dark times, we can focus on hope. Hope that we will smile. Hope that we will feel no pain. Hope that suffering will end. Because God says so.

God, thank you for tomorrow. Thank you, Lord, that the pain and hurt I feel now is not forever. Thank you that your hope is always within my reach.

A BEAUTIFUL GIFT

Be strong, and let your heart take courage,
all you who wait for the LORD.
PSALM 31:24 NRSV

When we find ourselves in a season of waiting, the wait can take a toll on our hearts and our faith, especially if it's intense and long. In these times, God gives us hope. Without it we could easily slip into doubt, discouragement, and even depression.

Hope is a beautiful gift. It makes trusting and expecting the best possible. It encourages us to get up every day with a positive attitude. Hope helps us look beyond today and believe in the impossible for tomorrow. Hope strengthens our faith and makes waiting possible.

Jesus, when life seems overwhelming, thank you that you are my hope. Thank you that in times of trouble you strengthen my hope so that I can patiently wait.

DEFINITION OF JUSTICE

*What does the Lord require of you? To act justly and
to love mercy and to walk humbly with your God.*

Micah 6:8 NIV

When someone wrongs us, we seek justice passionately. In
our anger, we want to see fairness played out and we demand
it at all cost. If justice is served, we figure we'll feel better.

What definition of justice are we demanding? God's?
Our own? Our definition of justice says, "You hurt me,
therefore, you should be repaid with an equal amount of
hurt." Or, "You hurt me, so you owe me something." God
tells us to act justly and to love mercy. We don't deserve
God's mercy, but he gives it freely. We can offer others that
same mercy. It's in God's definition of justice that we find
peace and healing.

*Lord, help me to love and treat those that hurt me in the
same way you treat me. Help me to let go of my pride and
need for justice, and see those that hurt me through your
eyes. Thank you for your justice that brings healing and
changes the world.*

LIST OF IMPERFECTIONS

You are altogether beautiful, my darling,
beautiful in every way.
SONG OF SOLOMON 4:7 NLT

Ask anyone what they'd change about themselves and they're quick to pull out a list of so-called imperfections. We may criticize our weight, size, smile, hair color, or height. We may think we are dull and without personality. We may wish to be more outgoing and outspoken or wonder why we aren't smarter, stronger, or wittier. We compare ourselves to our self-created definition of beauty, and we feel like we aren't enough.

But we are. God created each of us. If we could only see ourselves the way God sees us, we would know just how beautiful we really are. There is not a hair on our pretty little heads that he doesn't admire. He loves our heart and our soul. He is proud to call us his own. Believe it, because it is true.

God, sometimes I don't feel so beautiful. It's hard not to compare myself to others. When I do, I just feel terrible. Help me see myself the way you see me, beautiful and loved.

FRUIT OF SELF-CONTROL

The Holy Spirit produces this kind of fruit in our lives: love, joy, peace, patience, kindness, goodness, faithfulness, gentleness, and self-control.

GALATIANS 5:22-23 NLT

Self-control is like a muscle that needs exercise to be strengthened. We need self-control in our friendships, our finances, our health, our purity, and our emotions. Without that strong muscle, we could find ourselves in a whole heap of trouble. If we give in to our desires and emotions, we could very well hurt those around us with our actions and words. We also can deeply damage our own spirits, and separate ourselves from God.

Through discipline and focusing on Jesus, we can have self-control over every area in our lives. His Spirit in us produces in us the fruit of Spirit—self-control. He will give us the strength to hold strong when we feel weak.

God, I want my desires to line up with yours. In my weakness, it sometimes seems as if self-control escapes me. Help me to keep my focus on you. Help me to be disciplined in every area of my life, so I can live according to your will, not my emotions.

LIVING IN WORRY

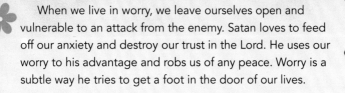

Cast your cares on the LORD and he will sustain you;
he will never let the righteous be shaken.

PSALM 55:22 NIV

When we live in worry, we leave ourselves open and vulnerable to an attack from the enemy. Satan loves to feed off our anxiety and destroy our trust in the Lord. He uses our worry to his advantage and robs us of any peace. Worry is a subtle way he tries to get a foot in the door of our lives.

Instead of dwelling on all of the what-ifs—all the things that could go wrong—we can focus on what God promises. That will protect our hearts from worry and the restlessness and fear that come along with it. Throwing all our cares on him, we can step into each day, confident in God's ability to take care of us.

Jesus, sometimes it's so easy for me to worry. I'm giving you all those cares. I want your peace to fill my heart and mind. Worry has no room in my heart.

APRIL

The LORD directs the steps of the godly.
He delights in every detail of their lives.
Though they stumble, they will never fall,
for the LORD holds them by the hand.

PSALM 37:23–24 NLT

SECOND CHANCE

"I will never again remember their sins and lawless deeds."
HEBREWS 10:17 TLB

Have you ever gone to bed at night just longing for a reset button? Maybe the day was just terrible, and you royally messed up. "If only I could start over again," you say.

You can. God's forgiveness gives you a new chance. Whether you ask forgiveness for a particular wrong or from a whole life of wrongs, he frees you from any mistakes. He doesn't keep a record of your wrongs. There is no list and no account to look back on. He is merciful and won't remind you of your shortcomings. God releases you of all sin and says that you are blameless. That's one grace-filled reset button.

God, I am so thankful that when I run to you for forgiveness, you give it freely. I am grateful that you cancel all of my debts. Thank you for each new day. Help me to embrace the new life you have given me.

TREASURED FRIEND

"I do not call you servants any longer, because the servant does not know what the master is doing; but I have called you friends, because I have made known to you everything that I have heard from my Father."

JOHN 15:15 NRSV

A friend is one of life's perfect gifts. A good friend spends hours with you and still can't get enough of your company. A good friend encourages you to become your very best. With a good friend, you feel included, wanted, and special. A good friend doesn't leave you out, and goes above and beyond to make sure that you feel loved. A good friend cares about every single detail of your life.

Jesus is that kind of friend. He loves you and wants to have a relationship with you. He wants to be a part of your everyday life. You bring him unspeakable joy. He can never get enough of your company. You are God's treasured friend.

God, I love being your friend. Your friendship brings me so much joy and comfort. Thank you for being my forever friend.

FAITH AND FEAR

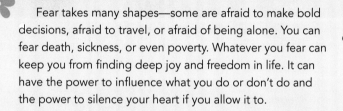

"You of little faith, why are you so afraid?"
Then he got up and rebuked the winds and
the waves, and it was completely calm.
MATTHEW 8:26 NIV

Fear takes many shapes—some are afraid to make bold decisions, afraid to travel, or afraid of being alone. You can fear death, sickness, or even poverty. Whatever you fear can keep you from finding deep joy and freedom in life. It can have the power to influence what you do or don't do and the power to silence your heart if you allow it to.

Jesus and his disciples were in the middle of a fierce storm when the disciples started to freak out. "Lord, save us!" they said. "We're going to drown!"

"Where's your faith?" Jesus asked. Then he simply calmed the wind and sea.

You see, faith is the opposite of fear. Fear says, "I don't believe God is able to take care of me." Faith says, "God is powerful and loving and always in control." Believing in God gives you courage because you realize God is who he says he is and he will do what he promised—he will be with you always.

Jesus, give me a heart filled with faith in your love and your
power. As I keep believing in you, grow my courage. Thank
you that you never leave me.

BEING REAL

*Clothe yourselves with humility toward one
another, because, "God opposes the proud
but shows favor to the humble."*
1 PETER 5:5 NIV

In a world that often demands perfection, one of the
hardest things to do is to be transparent with others. It's
difficult to open up and reveal not just the good parts about
ourselves but the broken parts that need attention and repair.

Authenticity is beautiful. When we can be real with
friends about our shortcomings and faults, we give them the
chance to usher in grace and compassion. We give them
the opportunity accept us and encourage us. We find close
friendships. Everyone struggles. We all have areas in our
lives that need to be dealt with. We don't need to pretend
to have it all together. Messy is ok. Messy is even beautiful.
Messy is where God can begin working in our lives.

*God, I want to live a life of authenticity. Help me set aside
my pride and my desire for perfection. Give me the courage
to be humble and bring to light the messy parts of me, so
that I can embrace your grace freely.*

ALL YOU HAVE

Always work enthusiastically for the Lord, for you know that nothing you do for the Lord is ever useless.
1 CORINTHIANS 15:58 NLT

Cutting corners usually seems like the easiest way out of a boring task or chore. If our hearts aren't in something, our efforts and energy can be easily affected. Following through diligently can be hard to achieve if what we're doing is tiring, boring, or seems like a waste of time. *Is it really worth all the work?* we might wonder.

Sticking to something you're not particularly excited about builds strong character. And whenever you do something, even if it's small and seemingly unimportant, treat it as if you are doing it for the Lord. Just pleasing the Lord can be a reward. When you're faithful in small things, it shows the Lord and others that you can be trusted with big things.

God, when I am tempted to be lazy and careless with a project, please redirect my heart. Help me to finish every single task well. I want to honor you every day in everything I do.

TOTALLY TRUST

Trust in the LORD with all your heart and lean
not on your own understanding;
in all your ways submit to him, and he
will make your paths straight.

PROVERBS 3:5-6 NIV

Don't try to figure everything out on your own. Don't put your hope in your connections, your abilities, or how you think something should work out.

Instead, trust in the Lord with everything you've got. Listen for his voice and what he thinks you should do. Trusting him, instead of doing things on your own, is always the easier path. He's well qualified to lead and guide you, and he will! He sees the whole picture. So though you may not understand how God is working in your life, you can have complete faith that he always is.

God, quiet my anxious and restless heart with your peace.
Thank you, Lord, that you are always at work and I can lean
on you.

BROKEN

*"Do not fear, for I have redeemed you; I have
summoned you by name; you are mine."*

ISAIAH 43:1 NIV

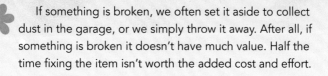

If something is broken, we often set it aside to collect
dust in the garage, or we simply throw it away. After all, if
something is broken it doesn't have much value. Half the
time fixing the item isn't worth the added cost and effort.

You might feel like you're too broken to be fixed, that
whatever you've done is too bad and that you're beyond
repair. You may feel too broken inside to be worth fighting
for. God thinks differently. God takes the broken and the
hurting and saves them. He sent Jesus to redeem you. That
means, he valued you so highly that he sent Jesus to die on
the cross. He loves you too much to set you aside.

*God, thank you for loving me so much you sent Jesus
to show your love. Thank you for seeing my value and
redeeming even the darkest and messiest parts of my life.*

THE TRUTH ABOUT YOU

*Truthful words stand the test of time,
but lies are soon exposed.*

PROVERBS 12:19 NLT

Lies. They can destroy friendships, harm family relationships, and cause deep pain in others. But telling ourselves lies can cause just as much harm. We might tell ourselves that we aren't worthy or lovable. We might tell ourselves that we are stupid, ugly, or unlikeable. Those lies can destroy our confidence and self-worth.

Compare whatever you tell yourself with what God says about you. You are a child of God. You are created in his image. He formed you inside your mother's womb. His thoughts about you are precious; they are more than the sand on the seashore. (Psalm 139:17, 18). Just like you should be truthful and honest to others, embrace truth about yourself.

Jesus, help me to speak truth not only to others but also to myself. Remind me to compare everything I say or think with the truth of your Word.

I CAN'T SEE YOU

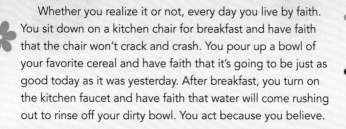

We live by faith, not by sight.
2 Corinthians 5:7 NIV

Whether you realize it or not, every day you live by faith. You sit down on a kitchen chair for breakfast and have faith that the chair won't crack and crash. You pour up a bowl of your favorite cereal and have faith that it's going to be just as good today as it was yesterday. After breakfast, you turn on the kitchen faucet and have faith that water will come rushing out to rinse off your dirty bowl. You act because you believe.

Saying you have faith is one thing. Actually living out faith is an entirely different matter. When you believe in God and are confident in his love, you'll act like it. If you think God is a provider, you'll be thankful instead of gripe about what you don't have. If you think God is love, you'll look for opportunities to donate food to a local food shelf, visit someone in the hospital, or serve others in practical ways. If you believe God is powerful, you won't stress out over things you've asked him to take care of. How do people see your faith?

God, I can't see you, but I know you're working in every situation. Help me to live, act, think, and talk about my faith.

THE PERFECT FIT

True godliness with contentment is itself great wealth.

1 TIMOTHY 6:6 NLT

In a culture where we're constantly bombarded with images of things that we want but don't have, things that we didn't know we needed but are told we do, and things society says we should have, it's easy to feel discontent.

True contentment doesn't come with having a nice house, a swimming pool, an iPhone, or even great friends. Real satisfaction comes from being true to yourself and living the way God intended you to. You were made in God's image, so walking in his ways is like slipping on the perfect size shoe. It fits right and feels right because it is.

Jesus, help me to be content with who I am and what I have. When I start to feel restless, help me find contentment in being with you and doing what's right.

THE RIGHT DIRECTION

They refused to listen; they forgot the
miracles you did for them.
So they became stubborn and turned against you,
choosing a leader to take them back to slavery.
But you are a forgiving God. You are kind and full of mercy.
You do not become angry quickly, and you have great love.
So you did not leave them.

NEHEMIAH 9:17 NCV

When we've done something wrong, we naturally distance ourselves from the people we've wronged. We might be afraid of a lecture or punishment. Maybe we just don't want to change and admit we are wrong. Or maybe we don't want to acknowledge our weakness. So we run away, oftentimes digging ourselves deeper into our mess.

Our relationship with God can look like that too. We attempt to hide ourselves from him because we are fearful of judgment or rejection. But God is kind. When we go to him and admit our failures, he meets us with kindness and grace. It doesn't mean there won't be a consequence to our sin, but he receives us with understanding and compassion. Rather than running from the one who loves us, we can run to him.

Jesus, sometimes my sin and shame keeps me from falling
at your feet. Gently remind me that you will not turn away.

BLESSING OF FRIENDS

Two people are better off than one, for they can help each
other succeed. If one person falls, the other can reach out
and help. But someone who falls alone is in real trouble.
ECCLESIASTES 4:9-10 NLT

Friends are one of God's greatest gifts. They bring joy,
encouragement, and companionship. Good friends bring out
the best in us and always point us toward Christ. True friends
aren't afraid to get messy with us. They know us at our best,
but also at our worst. They aren't put off by authenticity but
instead prefer it over a surface-level relationship.

God never intended for us to be alone. He created
this need in us to need each other and to love each other
deeply. God gave us friends so we can help each other
through life's tough times, knowing that there are plenty of
times when two people are better than one. If you are lonely
and need a friend, ask God to bring one into your life.

Lord, thank you for the blessing of wonderful friends. Thank
you for giving me friends to laugh with, cry with, and pray
with. Teach me how to love and serve my friends well.

OUTWARD FOCUS

Serve one another humbly in love.

GALATIANS 5:13 NIV

Don't you love it when someone says, "Here, let me help you," or "Can I do anything for you?" It's wonderful to be on the receiving end of servanthood. Being served gives us a sense of being loved and cared for. When we are going through time of sadness or discouragement, it can be hard to stop looking at our own needs and see the needs of others. Pain often makes us focus inward.

We learn to know God's love more deeply through serving. If we ask God to open our eyes to those hurting around us, he will. Pushing aside our own needs and problems and offering a helping hand to someone else will make our struggles fade. Serving others gives us a greater perspective—God's perspective—and brings us inexplicable joy. God uses us to show others how much they're loved, and then he fills us with purpose.

Lord, open my eyes and heart to those around me who are hurting. Use me as your servant to show them your love. Use me to bring others comfort and joy. May my own struggles teach me compassion and empathy.

PATIENCE IS THE KEY

With all humility and gentleness, with patience,
bearing with one another in love.

EPHESIANS 4:2 ESV

Living in relationship with others isn't always a walk in the park. We were all created differently, so we all have different personalities, likes, and dislikes. It is only natural that we will occasionally annoy each other. But it is possible to live in harmony with one another because God makes it possible.

Patience is the key to every strong relationship. When God tells us to "bear with one another in love," he's encouraging us to carry and love each other through thick and thin, regardless of our small differences and annoyances. Patience helps us hold our tongues and give encouragement rather than critique. Patience helps us set aside being right and care more about our friend being ok. Patience helps us work calmly and effectively through our issues. Patience keeps us from being easily offended and helps us to see another perspective. Patience is made possible because we choose to believe the best.

Jesus, just as you are patient with me, help me to be patient with others. Continue to teach me how to be a good friend.

FOOLPROOF PLANS

The LORD will fight for you,
and you shall hold your peace.
EXODUS 14:14 NKJV

Sometimes fear drives us to be micro managers of our lives. We're so afraid of what might happen that we take situations into our own hands and try to manipulate the outcome. Fear can cause us to act irrationally, and often that rash action only stirs up more trouble. When we do that, we forget that God is our defender. He fights on our behalf. He's got our best interests at heart. Every situation is under his control.

Instead of preparing to fight or micromanage, just trust. When we trust, we can go to God, wait patiently, and be still.

Lord, you are my defender. When fear tempts me to put my trust in my own strength and my own plans, remind me gently that your plans are foolproof. Still my anxious heart and quick hands. Help me to remain patiently in your care.

ARMS OPEN WIDE

He was despised and rejected—a man of
sorrows, acquainted with deepest grief.
ISAIAH 53:3 NLT

High school can feel like a popularity contest. Lines are clearly drawn in the sand defining who is popular, liked, and accepted. If you don't make the cut, it can be utterly devastating. Being rejected is one of the worst feelings. We feel like we're on the outside, aching for approval and acceptance. We all long to fit in. We all desire to belong, to have a place, to feel included.

Some of us don't feel like we belong anywhere. We don't fit in with our peers often because of our beliefs and life choices. We begin to wonder what is wrong with us and why no one loves us. If you find yourself in that hard place, Jesus will meet you there. He knows intimately what it's like to be rejected. In him you will always belong. When others turn their backs on you, he is there waiting, arms open wide. As a child of God, you belong, you have a family, and you have a place in God's home. When you seek to be with him, he won't turn you away. He loves you.

Lord, I feel at home with you. I feel wanted, loved, and
accepted. Your love comforts me and fills the loneliest
places of me.

UNEARNED RESPECT

Respect everyone, and love the family of
believers. Fear God, and respect the king.

1 PETER 2:17 NLT

Often we think respect needs to be earned before it's given. We demand that people prove their value to us before we treat them as valuable. But God wants us to give respect to everyone regardless of whether we believe they are worthy of it or not. That means listening to their stories, valuing their opinions whether we agree with them or not, and speaking well of them. In God's eyes, everyone is worthy of respect. Regardless of their heritage, their vocation, the color of their skin, or even their religious beliefs, they deserve to be treated with kindness, acceptance, esteem, and dignity.

That sweet teenage mother, the ninety-eight-year-old woman, the drug addict living on the street, the convict locked behind bars, and the annoying neighbor across the street. We should treat them all as if they hold great value. Because they do. And so do you. Despite what you might have been told, you too are worthy of respect. In God's eyes you are valuable and worthy. Your stories are important and should be told. Your opinions are worth being shared. You matter.

Lord, show me how to hold people in high esteem. Help me
to set aside my pride, my opinions, and embrace people
that cross my path. Help me to see others the way that you
see them—valuable and worthy of respect.

LOVE YOUR ENEMIES

"You have heard that it was said, 'Love your neighbor and hate your enemy.' But I tell you, love your enemies and pray for those who persecute you."
MATTHEW 5:43-44 NIV

Love your enemies? Pray for them? Really? How? Sometimes we feel justified to hate someone or be angry. But God says we *must* love others. While this may seem impossible, Jesus gave us our greatest example of love. Even when he was being beaten, persecuted, and hated, he begged God to have mercy on his killers. His love allowed him to see deeper than their actions. He saw beyond their anger and looked directly into their hearts. His love for them moved him to compassion and grace.

To choose to love someone who is against us and who has harmed us is one of the hardest commandments. It requires humility to put our anger and hate aside, get down on our knees, and *pray for* our enemies. Hard? Yes. But it's not impossible. Not with God.

Lord, I want to love my enemies the way you love them. Move me to compassion and take away my pride. May my love for you lead me to love those around me deeply, even those that hurt me.

WITHIN MARRIAGE

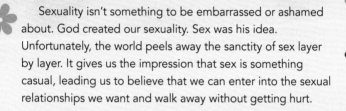

A man leaves his father and mother and is joined
to his wife, and the two are united into one.

GENESIS 2:24 NLT

Sexuality isn't something to be embarrassed or ashamed about. God created our sexuality. Sex was his idea. Unfortunately, the world peels away the sanctity of sex layer by layer. It gives us the impression that sex is something casual, leading us to believe that we can enter into the sexual relationships we want and walk away without getting hurt.

It's simply not true. Sex outside of marriage ruins our view of it and brings heartache. Sex inside the context of marriage brings joy and life. God created sex to be between a husband and a wife, to bring unity and oneness to their marriage. It binds them together through intimacy and trust. Sex within marriage is beautiful, sacred, special, and worth waiting for.

Thank you Jesus for creating my sexuality. Thank you that I don't have to feel embarrassed or ashamed about the way you made my body. Help me honor you by protecting my body, not taking it for granted or abusing its purpose. Give me the strength and patience to wait for the gift of sex inside marriage.

THE GOOD PATH

*"Enter through the narrow gate. For wide is the gate
and broad is the road that leads to destruction, and
many enter through it. But small is the gate and narrow
the road that leads to life, and only a few find it."*

MATTHEW 7:13-14 NIV

There are two paths in life. One is wide and easy to find.
One is narrow and there are only a few that find it. One
leads toward God, and the other path leads toward death.
Doing what we want, when we want, how we want, and
with whomever we want seems to be the easier route to go.
That's what the enemy would like us to think. Satan wants us
to doubt God's goodness and strength. He'd like us to think
that we aren't smart enough, good enough, strong enough,
or devoted enough to walk in God's ways. He toys with our
emotions and our weaknesses because he wants us to quit.

Doing what God asks may seem constraining, but it
actually brings peace and incredible joy. It isn't always easy
but it comes with unbelievable reward. When the road gets
difficult, tiring, and long, we should press closer into God.
He will give us the strength to continue and carry us through.

*Thank you, Lord, that though your path is narrow, it's safe
and good and best. Thank you for your unfailing grace and
for always catching me when I am about to slip and fall.*

GUILTY OR NOT

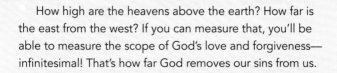

As high as the heavens are above the earth,
so great is his love for those who fear him;
as far as the east is from the west,
so far has he removed our transgressions from us.
PSALM 103:11-12 NIV

How high are the heavens above the earth? How far is the east from the west? If you can measure that, you'll be able to measure the scope of God's love and forgiveness—infinitesimal! That's how far God removes our sins from us.

As believers, guilt has no place in our lives. Yet it ever so quietly attempts to make our lives its home. It stops us from moving past sin and into the arms of Jesus. It keeps us from stepping into complete healing and restoration. Focusing on regret actually stops us from living in grace. God doesn't want us to be weighed down with guilt or wrapped up in self-condemnation. If you are battling guilt—stop! It is not worth your time and energy. Instead believe in the bigness and greatness of God who freely forgives you.

When I make a mistake, God, guilt seems to pull me down.
Thank you that when you wash away my sins, you also free
me from guilt and condemnation.

CONNECTION

You make known to me the path of life;
in your presence there is fullness of joy.
PSALM 16:11 ESV

Have you ever had a conversation with someone and walked away feeling like that person never heard what you had to say? Sometimes we're so distracted with media that we actually fail to connect with the person sitting right beside us.

We all long to connect with others on a deep level and talk about what's really important. That describes how God feels about spending time with us. God is always willing and ready to be with us. But sometimes we get caught up in being busy. If we put down our gadgets, quiet our hearts, and take turns speaking and listening, we discover what it means to have a deeper relationship with him.

Jesus, thank you that you enjoy my company. I'd like to enjoy your company more too. Time with you is refreshing and exactly what my soul needs.

DECISIONS

"The gatekeeper opens the gate for him, and the sheep hear his voice. He calls his own sheep by name and leads them out. When he has brought out all his own, he goes ahead of them, and the sheep follow him because they know his voice."

JOHN 10:3-4 NRSV

What should I wear? Who should I invite to my party? How do I study for this exam? Where should I go to college? As we grow up, the decisions get bigger and bigger. Some of those decisions seem exciting and others overwhelming. Afraid of making the wrong decision, we sometimes find ourselves stalling, not quite sure what to do.

God doesn't leave us alone to figure everything out for ourselves. He's like a shepherd who leads us. Knowing him and hearing his voice is key to knowing which direction to take and what decision to make. Following his voice, we'll never go wrong.

Thank you, Jesus, for being a good shepherd and telling me where to go. Help me to listen to your voice and learn to know it well, so I can be confident that I'm walking in the right direction.

PLAYING THE PART

People with integrity walk safely,
but those who follow crooked paths will slip and fall.

PROVERBS 10:9 NLT

We can all fake good character. We can play the part of a good Christian: go to church, read the Bible, and follow the rules when people are watching. But what choices do we make when we're alone? Do we consistently do what is honorable and right even when there is no reward, even when no one is watching? Do we cheat if we know we won't get caught? Do we cut corners instead of doing our very best?

Integrity, not hypocrisy, is what God wants for us. The Lord sees through all our attempts to be something we aren't, so pretending with him is a waste of time. He would rather we be upfront and honest. Not only will our relationship with him improve but the rewards with others will come too. People will learn to trust our words and depend on our character.

God, I want to be the same person in private as I am when surrounded by others. I long to live a life of integrity and honesty. Point out any hypocrisy in my life so I can live with good character.

WHAT ABOUT ME

"Rise and stand upon your feet, for I have appeared to you for this purpose, to appoint you as a servant and witness to the things in which you have seen me and to those in which I will appear to you."

ACTS 26:16 ESV

From the time you were little, parents and grandparents, teachers and friends probably asked you, "What do you want to be when you grow up?" Someday you might grow up to preach in front of thousands, or find a cure for a deadly disease, or build an orphanage in Africa.

Sometimes defeat and self-doubt worm their way into your life, and you might begin to wonder if your life has meaning and purpose. It can seem as though others are called to great and amazing things, and you are left wondering, *What about me?* Right now, your calling is pretty simple: study hard, listen to your parents, love others, serve others, and make an impact in everyday ways. Your calling may seem small in your eyes, but to God there is great purpose even in the little things that don't bring a lot of fanfare. You are an important part of his plan, so embrace every day and impact people in the ways that you can.

God, keep me from wasting my time and energy searching out a bigger, more important calling. Help me seize the calling you've given me today—to love and serve those around me.

MANAGING PRIORITIES

Remember your Creator in the days of your youth.
Ecclesiastes 12:1 NIV

Managing school, sports, activities, and maybe even a part-time job can feel exhausting. Each day brings a set of problems to solve and expectations to meet. In the middle of a busy season, it is easy to feel like we are alone, that no one can possibly understand the strain and stress we are under. We want to live a life well for God but at the end of the day we feel drained with nothing else to give.

There is only so much we can handle in one day. God understands that. But he asks us to put him first. When that priority is set, the others just fall into place. As we do the other things throughout our day, he'll renew and refresh us. When we feel depleted, he supports us.

God, thank you that when life seems like too much,
you are there to help me face another day.
Remind me to put you first and depend more on you
and less on my abilities and strength.

BEAUTIFUL HUMILITY

Humble yourselves before the Lord, and he will lift you up.
JAMES 4:10 NIV

Humbling ourselves and admitting we're wrong or have made a mistake can be a hard pill to swallow. Acknowledging our weaknesses and exposing ourselves to judgment and scrutiny can be even harder. Pride keeps us distant from God and others. When we are proud, we rob people of the chance to love us despite our brokenness, despite our mistakes. Pride makes us hard and unchangeable. If we are proud, we leave no room for growth.

Humility, though, can be such a beautiful thing. Humility restores broken relationships and brings us closer to God. The more humble we are, the more we are made aware of God's grace, mercy, and love in our lives. Humbling ourselves gives us the chance to change for the better.

God, it's never easy for me to admit I'm wrong. I need your grace and mercy to change me. Replace my pride with meekness. May I always be aware of how desperately I need you. I'd rather run confidently into your arms than wallow in my pride.

DO THE IMPOSSIBLE

The Lord is my strength and shield.
I trust him with all my heart.
He helps me, and my heart is filled with joy.

PSALM 28:7 NLT

Have you ever set your heart on doing something only to be discouraged by the careless words of others? They may have felt that you were inexperienced or ill-equipped. Sometimes people have good intentions but aren't particularly helpful.

Too often we let other's disbelief in our abilities keep us from pursuing our biggest dreams and desires—desires that God has planted in our hearts. If they think we can't, then we shouldn't, right? Wrong. Often God calls us to do things that seem bigger than ourselves. Sometimes he calls us to do the impossible because he believes in our abilities. Other times he calls us to do the impossible because he wants us to lean on him. Instead of letting self-doubt grow, our confidence should be in him.

God, help me place my confidence in you, not in the
opinion of others or the circumstances around me.

STICKS AND STONES

*"Listen to me, you who know right from wrong,
you who cherish my law in your hearts. Do not be
afraid of people's scorn, nor fear their insults."*

ISAIAH 51:7 NLT

We all want to be liked, accepted, and loved by others. However, some people demand a cost for their affection and approval: a cost that may conflict with our morals, values, and beliefs. We are tempted to give into peer pressure, even while knowing our choices may hurt God. On the other hand, if we choose to walk away from approval and reject what our peers want us to do, it may mean facing serious criticism.

"Stick and stones may break my bones but words will never hurt me," goes the nursery rhyme. Not exactly. Words *do* hurt. Being made fun of *does* sting. "Don't be afraid of people's scorn," God says. Why? In the end, those who throw around insults will be shown to be wrong. God's way will last forever. So stick to what's right and surround yourselves with friends that will respect and encourage your choice to honor God. Criticism can be brutal, but it can't take away your peace. It won't change what's right.

*Jesus, sometimes my need for others' approval is
overwhelming. Please surround me with loving,
wise friends who support my decisions to honor you.*

REAL BEAUTY

Don't be concerned about the outward beauty of fancy hairstyles, expensive jewelry, or beautiful clothes. You should clothe yourselves instead with the beauty that comes from within, the unfading beauty of a gentle and quiet spirit, which is so precious to God.

1 PETER 3:3-4 NLT

Magazines, billboards, celebrities, and media all try to convince us what the standard of beauty is. If we fall short, plenty of people are ready to swoop in and benefit from our lack of self-worth. They sell us cosmetics, clothes, gym memberships, and even plastic surgery to satisfy our desire to be beautiful. No matter how much we spend, though, it's a goal we never seem to reach.

Real beauty isn't something you can purchase and put on. Real beauty is not the brand of makeup you apply or the designer clothes you wear. Real beauty comes from within. The beauty of a gentle and quiet spirit never fades. That kind of beauty, says God, is precious—just like you are.

Lord, please continue to work in my heart. Make me into a woman that is kind, gracious, and loving. Help me to care less about my outward appearance and focus more on what really matters. Thank you for showing me what real beauty is.

MAY

We know that all things
work together for good
to those who love God,
to those who are the called
according to His purpose.

ROMANS 8:28 NKJV

GREATNESS

God thunders wondrously with his voice;
he does great things that we cannot comprehend.

JOB 37:5 ESV

We all have dreams for what we want out of life. Most of us aspire to greatness, even though we can't see how it will happen. Greatness cannot grow on its own; true greatness comes from God. That's because God is the one who is great.

His voice commands the thunder, creates light, and dawns the day. It's through his strength that our lives will count for something greater than we can imagine. Put your life in his hands. Allow him to speak to your soul. And watch what he will do with your life.

God, you know that I desire greatness. I look around me and I see that everyone is living for something—some of it matters and some of it doesn't. But I want to live a life that is set apart. Marked by your call. Use me to do great things.

BEAUTY THAT LASTS

Charm is deceptive, and beauty does not last;
but a woman who fears the Lord will be greatly praised.
PROVERBS 31:30 NLT

The campaign to love yourself is everywhere today. "Be-YOU-tiful". Be who you are. Shake off the haters and just do you. But the truth of the matter is that even with all this encouragement to be yourself, it has never been harder to do so.

Social media has brought with it the age of the filter. We can look tanner, thinner, and even apply make-up all with a few swipes. How can we be truly content with who we are when it's so easy to alter the way others see us? Maybe it's because we don't have the right definition of beauty. If beauty is what makes us desirable, to whom are we desirable?

What God desires is a woman who fears him. Not the hide-under-the-table kind of fear but a respect-and-reverence kind of fear. That's what he finds beautiful, and it's a beauty that lasts—forever.

Thank you Lord for loving me for who I am. I know outward beauty isn't bad; it just doesn't last.

YOLO

If they plant to satisfy their sinful selves, their sinful selves will bring them ruin. But if they plant to please the Spirit, they will receive eternal life from the Spirit.
GALATIANS 6:8 NCV

YOLO—You Only Live Once—right? So why not do whatever you feel like doing? Why not take a chance, make a mistake or two?

The truth is we don't only live for now—we have an eternity ahead of us. What we do now affects what happens later. If we focus only on living for right now, on satisfying our desires to sin, then the result will be total ruin. But if we live in a way that pleases God, our promise is eternal life. Shifting our focus to live for the long run means evaluating the decisions and lifestyle we live now.

God, keep me mindful of eternity. Remind me that I'm not just living for myself or for right now, but I have an everlasting future in your presence.

FINDING THE WAY BACK

Repent and return, so that your sins may be wiped away, in order that times of refreshing may come from the presence of the Lord.

ACTS 3:19 NASB

Arguments and gossip can divide friendships. In the same way, sin divides us from God. It creates distance between us. That's because God is holy. Sin makes him sad because it means we can't be near him. We can't stand in his presence when we have grieved his heart.

Separation from him, though, doesn't have to be permanent. Because he loved us so much, he provided a way back to relationship with him through grace. Finding our way back into his presence and into his forgiveness is as simple as reaching out and asking for it. What he asks for is a genuine heart of apology and the willingness to return to him. Telling him we're sorry and asking his forgiveness, we welcome him to refresh us with his presence and to redeem us with his grace.

Lord Jesus, when I do things I know aren't pleasing to you, my instinct is to run. I don't want to stand before you ashamed. Clean me from the stain of my sin and make me new again in your eyes.

OWE LOVE

Owe no one anything, except to love one another;
for the one who loves another has fulfilled the law.

ROMANS 13:8 NRSV

If someone owed you money, you'd be sure to say, "Pay up!" The Bible says we all owe a big debt—that debt is love. Sometimes love comes easily. But many times, real Christ-like love is hard. When we look at people, we tend to see their imperfections, their sin, their mess. That can make loving difficult.

Jesus had the incredible ability to look at people and see them separate from their sin. He knew his grace and forgiveness was enough for whatever mess they were in. That made it easier for him to love. Only when we take his point of view—that what Christ has done for us he's done for others as well—will we be able to love like Jesus did.

Jesus, help me see the world through your eyes. I know that my vision is flawed and that my heart isn't capable of loving others without you. Fill me up with your compassion and your grace, so that I'll be able to give others what I owe them—love.

NOT YOUR MASTER

*Sin is no longer your master, for you no longer
live under the requirements of the law. Instead,
you live under the freedom of God's grace.*

ROMANS 6:14 NLT

Sin can be a controlling force in our lives. We can fight to
be done with it, but still be frustrated with how easily we fall
right back into a pattern of shame and defeat. The reality is
that as long as we try to fight sin in our own strength, we'll
never be free of it.

God can do what we can't. Only through *his* strength
and what *Jesus* did on the cross, can we stop being a
slave to sin. Maybe there is sin in your life that has been
mastering you. If so, know that there is freedom for you in
Christ. Determine in your heart to detach yourself from that
sin and everything that it represents in your life. Call on the
Lord and ask him to make that a reality.

*God, I want to live a pure life. I don't want to be trapped
in sin that keeps me from you. Help me to be more than a
conqueror through your strength.*

LIVING NOW

For still the vision awaits its appointed time;
it hastens to the end—it will not lie.
If it seems slow, wait for it;
it will surely come; it will not delay.

HABAKKUK 2:3 ESV

The growing up years can feel like a holding pattern.
You're standing right on the brink of your whole life, but it's
still just out of reach. It's easy to start wishing away the time
and looking ahead to when your future will really start.

But all we really have in life is the present moment. None
of us are promised tomorrow. If we spend our days planning
for the future, then we'll look back and see only a list of plans
instead of a life well lived. God wants to use us right now, as
we are. He doesn't ask us to change, grow up, get married,
or get older before he can use us. He asks us to embrace
today, this moment, and obey him with our whole heart.

Offer your life up to God, as it is, and let him take care of
the details. He will create for you the most beautiful life.

God, I want to live for you right now. Help me to give you
every moment. I want to live my life with your vision and
your purpose.

137

THE BEST PATH

*Your word is a lamp for my feet,
a light on my path.*
PSALM 119:105 NIV

*Hmm. Should I have chocolate cake or carrot cake?
Should I wear jeans or sweats?*

Life is full of decisions, some of them more important
than others. For some of the more critical decisions, it
can be hard to tell which direction to go or which choice
to make. We can get advice from all sorts of sources, but
sometimes it's hard to know who to really listen to.

In a world of choices, our one true reliable road map is
the Bible. God's Word has been time tested and repeatedly
proven again and again. We might not think it has answers
for our specific issues. If we pray and ask God to speak to
us, we'll find direction that is more anchored than any other
we consider.

*Heavenly Father, I want to be guided by your truth. I know
I'm going to be continually faced with choices. I want to
make sure that in every decision I'm seeking your wisdom
and comparing my choices with what your Word says.*

SOMEONE TO TURN TO

My soul, wait silently for God alone,
For my expectation is from Him.
He only is my rock and my salvation;
He is my defense;
I shall not be moved.

PSALM 62:5-6 NKJV

We were created for dependency. We need others.
When we are going through a struggle, we want to have
someone to turn to. We need help bearing our burdens—
they weigh us down so heavily. If we can share that weight
with even just one other person, it lightens our load.

Though we're thankful for good friends, sometimes
people are going to fail us. There's no way around that
truth, and no exception to that rule. God, the creator of the
universe, has never failed and never will. He is our rock and
our salvation. Troubles threaten to knock us down, but with
God's help we can stand firm no matter what life throws our
way. Train yourself to run to the Lord when you need help.
He will rescue you; he will never fail you.

I need your strength Lord. I'm used to running to others
when I need help, but I know the true source of my salvation
lies with you. Teach me to turn to you.

MY LIFE

Sanctify them in the truth;
Your word is truth.
JOHN 17:17 NASB

So much of this season of our lives is about preparation. We're constantly preparing for something—for graduation, for college, for a career. We're looking forward, and we want to be ready for whatever lies ahead.

As we lay the groundwork for our lives, we can't exclude the best thing—God's Word, which is truth. If it's not woven throughout our life's plan, then everything we've worked for amounts to nothing in eternity. In his Word we will find the key to so many of our questions, to our peace, to our being worth something. Take hold of God's truth. Learn to long for his wisdom. Open his Word every morning. Take in what he has for you and weave it in to your life until you can't go a day without it.

Teach me to love the Bible, Lord. I don't want to do life without your wisdom; I need your truth. Speak to me and help me be excited to open your Word.

VALUED ADVICE

Listen, my son, to your father's instruction
and do not forsake your mother's teaching.
They are a garland to grace your head
and a chain to adorn your neck.
PROVERBS 1:8-9 NIV

Listening to what our parents have to say isn't always easy. After all, we see their flaws. When you've seen someone at their worst, they can lose some credibility. It's easier to respect people who aren't so close—who you've never seen lose their cool or be unfair.

Parents aren't perfect. But when you stop and think about what life might look like from your parents' perspective, it can turn your whole world upside down. They've lived through many of the things you're going through. They have a lot of life experience. And they love you. Listen to what they have to say. Hear their wisdom, and accept it as added value to your life.

Dear God, respecting my parents doesn't always come naturally. Sometimes I get frustrated with them. But you chose them as my parents for a reason. I know that they love me and want what's best for me. Change my attitude and teach me to accept their advice.

BEFORE YOU SPEAK

*Those who are careful about what they say
keep themselves out of trouble.*
PROVERBS 21:23 NCV

Shoot off a quick text. Post a quick tweet. Make a casual comment. It's easy to do any of these without giving much thought to what we're putting out there. Many times, we do it out of a reaction to what someone else said. We're mostly concerned with painting ourselves in the best possible light. We forget, though, that everything we say has an effect on the ones who hear or see it. That impact can be positive, but it can also be negative.

Before you communicate, do you consider how it will affect people? Next time, take a minute first. Consider the potential impact of your words and ask, "Is what I'm about to do going to be beneficial or potentially harmful?"

Lord, help me think before I speak. I don't want to mindlessly put my words out there; I want them to have purpose. I can impact people with what I say, and I don't want to abuse that power. Give me wisdom and restraint when I speak.

VALUE OF KINDNESS

Be kind to each other, tenderhearted, forgiving one another, just as God through Christ has forgiven you.

EPHESIANS 4:32 NLT

Kindness is always worth something. Meanness may come more easily at times, but it's never the right choice. We can't know the full picture by just looking at someone. We have no idea what's going on in their lives. Everyone has a story. Everyone has issues, struggles, and hurts. The reality is that the only safe bet is to be kind. Simply put: treat others as you want to be treated. Smile, be friendly, and be caring. Better yet, find out what someone's story is.

The reality is that *you* don't always deserve kindness. Sometimes you act in a way that isn't worthy of someone's best. But Christ gives you his best always. He always loves you, forgives you, and comforts you. There's no mistake in being kind. By showing kindness to others, you will always be doing what's right.

Thank you, Jesus, for your kindness. Help me think past my own circumstances and recognize that everyone has a story. I know that kindness is never the wrong reaction to someone. Help it to always be my first.

FATHER TO THE FATHERLESS

*Father of orphans and protector of widows
is God in his holy habitation.*
PSALM 68:5 NRSV

Everyone has a biological father and a biological mother. That's just how it is. But while everyone has biological parents, the relationship with those parents can be very different. Not all of us are blessed to have parents who are involved in our lives. Whether it's divorce, death, or disconnection that robbed us of it, absence of parents is a difficult reality that we have to live with.

God promises to be a father to the fatherless. He steps in to fill the void for the broken. He loves, even when only lack of love has been known. He comforts where pain has been inflicted. He stays with those who have been left behind. Where there has been abandonment and hurt, he is faithful with his tender love.

Thank you, Father, that you heal the parts of my heart that are hurting. Thank you that even in the areas where my parents have failed me, you have restored me.

LOVING JUSTICE

"For I, the LORD, love justice;
I hate robbery and wrongdoing.
In my faithfulness I will reward my people
and make an everlasting covenant with them."

ISAIAH 61:8 NIV

There are some things in the world we just can't make sense of. Things we wonder why God hasn't put a stop to. Wrongs we want to make right. Things we wish we could fix or change, or even just erase.

Every time you wonder why evil exists, remember that grace does also. Whatever saddens and breaks your heart is even more troubling to the God who created the world for his glory. He longs for justice more than you ever will; and he will absolutely have his way. God is faithful—don't forget that when you see the evidence of faithless people. He promises to protect you, shield you, and love you. He won't let evil have the final say.

Thank you, God, for being just. Thank you that I can trust your heart for the world. Thank you for your grace for us. Please bring peace to my heart, even when there's chaos in the world.

THE GOOD WIFE

An excellent wife, who can find?
For her worth is far above jewels.
PROVERBS 31:10 NASB

Why do you think a good wife isn't easy to find? More importantly, what do you think an "excellent" wife is?

Marriage is a life-long commitment. While it isn't always easy, marriage is one of the greatest gifts God gives. Though being a wife and being married may seem a long way off, you can start preparing now. Purposefully grow yourself in grace, in forgiveness, and in humility. Keep your heart free from entanglement with other loves. Practice forgiveness. Become a natural at apologizing. Learn to speak with kindness, even when you want to speak in anger. Let your heart be guided by the Lord, and trust that he will give you a great marriage in a world of so many broken ones.

God, I know that I can trust you with my heart and my future marriage. You created love and want us to love one another in a way that reflects the love you have for the world. Do a work in my heart now so that my marriage will forever reap the benefits.

ALL YOUR LOVE

I hold this against you:
You have forsaken the love you had at first.
REVELATION 2:4 NIV

When you first come to God, you give him all of your heart. Your love is whole, passionate, and honest. As time goes on, other loves become tempting to you. You begin to divide your devotion to God by looking to others, and it hinders your relationship with him.

Always keep yourself going back to the love you had for God at first. Remind yourself what it felt like when your heart first said yes to him. Nothing and no one in this world is worth loving the way that he is. No one else will love you in return with as much passion, grace, and constant love. No one else is worth all of your love.

God, I remember what it felt like when I first said yes to following you. My love was sincere, complete, and pure. Since then I've gotten distracted by other things that so easily pull me away. Help me to keep my heart completely focused on you.

KNOW YOUR HEART

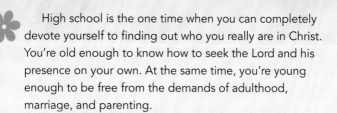

You have searched me, LORD,
and you know me.
PSALM 139:1 NIV

High school is the one time when you can completely devote yourself to finding out who you really are in Christ. You're old enough to know how to seek the Lord and his presence on your own. At the same time, you're young enough to be free from the demands of adulthood, marriage, and parenting.

Use this time to explore who you are, what you like, what you're good at, and the gifts that God has placed in you. Take advantage of this time to discover the extent of your heart. As a result, when you are ready to give your heart and love away to another person, you will be able to say with confidence that you know exactly what you are giving. Know your own heart—and come to know it through the God who created it.

Lord, help me discover more of who you've created me to be. Help me to give my love away when it is the right time— after I have come to know my heart and all that you created me to be.

STAY CLOSE

*Dear friends, let us love one another, for love
comes from God. Everyone who loves has
been born of God and knows God.*

1 JOHN 4:7 NIV

It's a simple principle: The closer an object is to a light
source, the more illuminated that object will become. Stay
close to the light of Christ, let him shine through you. Draw
your love from him. Without being connected to him as your
source, your light will go out and you will find yourself empty.

When our love comes from God, who is love, it is being
replenished every time we step into his presence. He loves
others through us, and he will never run out of love to give.
Always love—above everything else. Love Christ first, and
then those around you. The moment you begin to love
others more than you love Christ is the very moment your
light will go out.

*Love through me, God. Shine your light through me. I'm too
weak to do life on my own. I have to be connected to you as
my strength, my light, and my love.*

BRING HIM JOY

Let us hear the conclusion of the whole matter:
Fear God and keep His commandments,
For this is man's all.

ECCLESIASTES 12:13 NKJV

Our highest achievements in life won't be fame or fortune, even though those things might be nice. Instead, the greatest thing we can do is to make God proud. When we search out what God loves, we'll soon discover that one of God's greatest desires is for our lives to bring glory to his name, through love and worship of him. He wants for us to be holy, just like he is holy. Why? So that we can be with him.

We are God's creation. What could be better than bringing joy to the one who created us? We bring him joy by loving him and keeping his commands.

God, help me to learn what it is you love so that I can bring you joy. If there is anything in my life that saddens you, show me what it is. I am your masterpiece, your child, and I just want to bring you glory. Teach me how.

PATHS OF RIGHTEOUSNESS

He guides me in the paths of righteousness
For His name's sake.

PSALM 23:3 NASB

Why do you think God leads us in paths of righteousness? Why does he want us to do good? He leads us in these ways because his name is great. His name is the greatest name—the name above all names. If you identify yourself as a Christian, then you are associating yourself with Christ. If you link yourself to him, then you are declaring to the world that you are a representative of his ways.

We need to act in a way that brings glory to God, and that shows the world how great and loving he truly is. If we live in a way that drags his name through the mud, we would not only misrepresent his name but rob people of the opportunity to know how incredible he is. Remember, as you interact with others, that you are representing the Lord to them. Do your best to do it well.

Thank you God, for leading me in paths of righteousness. Help me to represent you well to the people I come in contact with. I want to show your love to them.

FROM SOMEONE ELSE

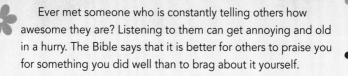

Let someone else praise you, not your own mouth—
a stranger, not your own lips.
PROVERBS 27:2 NLT

Ever met someone who is constantly telling others how awesome they are? Listening to them can get annoying and old in a hurry. The Bible says that it is better for others to praise you for something you did well than to brag about it yourself.

There is always more satisfaction when others take notice of us on their own than when we work to make them notice us. One person who notices is Jesus. Who better to be praised by? The day is coming soon when he will look at those people who have loved and obeyed him and reward them. Instead of bragging about yourself, give praise and glory to Jesus.

Lord, help me not to brag. Instead, help me to look for ways to please you. I want your recognition more than anyone else's.

LIKE A MIST

You do not know what will happen tomorrow! Your life is like a mist. You can see it for a short time, but then it goes away.

JAMES 4:14 NCV

Life can feel like it's spinning around you. You wish you could just catch it in your hand and hold on to it for a moment, long enough to take a good look. We do our best to plan, but in many ways life is an unpredictable adventure. It takes what you are and shapes who you become. It is both the platform to succeed as well as the beautiful chance to make mistakes and learn.

In the end, our life is short. It's like a mist that settles thick in the early morning but evaporates in the morning sun. In the context of eternity, it's the blink of an eye. So make it count. Do something with your life that will outlive you. Don't focus on joining the rat race. Focus on changing the world—and make a change that will last long after you've made it.

God, my life is everything to me—but it shouldn't be. You should be everything to me because you are the only one who can take my temporary life and make an eternal impact out of it. Lead me to live in a way that makes a difference.

WANDERER

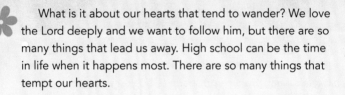

Sensible people keep their eyes glued on wisdom,
but a fool's eyes wander to the ends of the earth.
PROVERBS 17:24 NLT

What is it about our hearts that tend to wander? We love the Lord deeply and we want to follow him, but there are so many things that lead us away. High school can be the time in life when it happens most. There are so many things that tempt our hearts.

These years can be difficult, but they can also be some of the best! Stay strong. Remember that you are God's child, and he knows you by name. He's jealous for the hearts of his children; he doesn't want to share you with anything or anyone else that would harm you. So hold fast to his love. Don't allow the things in this world to make you wander. Be one of the few who chooses to keep their eyes glued on wisdom, and spend every moment you can living your best in his love.

God, help me never wander from you. I know that nothing this world has to offer will ever bring me as much joy as you do. Keep me close, Lord.

VOICE OF CONVICTION

*My guilt has overwhelmed me
like a burden too heavy to bear.*

PSALM 38:4 NIV

Do you ever have moments where your conscience won't leave you alone? You've said some nasty things about someone, or you looked at something you shouldn't have, and it doesn't sit well in your heart.

God cares enough about you to bring conviction and the Holy Spirit's nudging. His objective is for you to repent because, until you do, your sin will cause a wall between you and him. God cannot stand separation with you, so he will do whatever it takes to break down what gets in the way of your relationship. When you begin to feel that conviction come over you, respond to it quickly and with a humble heart.

Keep my heart soft toward you, Lord. I don't want to ignore your Holy Spirit. Sometimes I try to push away that voice of conviction, but I want instead to be thankful that you're willing to make our relationship right.

FOREVER LOVE

Give thanks to the Lord, for he is good,
for his steadfast love endures forever.
Psalm 136:1 esv

We see a lot of love that doesn't last long. People get together, claim to be in love, and then want nothing to do with each other a few months or years later.

There is one love that is promised to us for eternity. One love that will never change, never lessen, and never be removed. God promises us his love forever—and God never breaks his promises. He loves you for always. Not just for days when you look pretty. Not just for moments when you're good. Not just for the times you obey him and please him. For always. No conditions. No exceptions. Just pure, complete, eternal love.

Thank you, Jesus, for loving me unconditionally. Thank you that in a world of less than perfect love, yours is perfect. I want to love you more each day. Cause my heart to respond to your love and to feel it.

A LIVING SACRIFICE

Therefore, I urge you, brothers and sisters, in view of God's mercy, to offer your bodies as a living sacrifice, holy and pleasing to God—this is your true and proper worship.

ROMANS 12:1 NIV

Sacrifice. It's not a very comfortable word is it? What does it mean to be a living sacrifice? As God's followers and children, we should live in a way that honors and blesses him. It is so difficult to live that kind of life with all of the temptations of this world and everything at our fingertips. In fact, we can't live a holy and pleasing life *and* give into temptation. We fall into the trap of doing what we want: buying too much stuff, dressing to fit in, gossiping about others, being ungrateful—and these are just a few things we need to watch out for.

If you practice each week to work on an area in your life that you feel hasn't blessed the Lord, then you will feel something change, and you'll receive the confidence that only your Heavenly Father can give. By living this way, you are sacrificing your desires and truly worshiping him. *That* is pleasing to God.

God, help me to sacrifice the things that I want in order to serve you and live the way you want me to live. I know it is better for me to live your way, so help me continue to choose that.

HIS MERCY

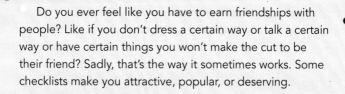

Then he saved us—not because we were good
enough to be saved but because of his kindness
and pity—by washing away our sins and giving
us the new joy of the indwelling Holy Spirit.

TITUS 3:5 TLB

Do you ever feel like you have to earn friendships with people? Like if you don't dress a certain way or talk a certain way or have certain things you won't make the cut to be their friend? Sadly, that's the way it sometimes works. Some checklists make you attractive, popular, or deserving.

God doesn't operate that way. We didn't do a thing to earn his salvation. God saves us because of his love for us. There's nothing we did to earn it. There is so much freedom in realizing that. When we know that his mercy has never been about what we do, we learn to relax and accept it.

Thank you, God, that I don't have to earn your mercy or
your salvation. You are so good to me. I'm so thankful for
your mercy. In a world where I have to prove myself again
and again, you're merciful just because that's who you are,
not because of anything I do.

COMFORTED

"They are blessed who grieve, for God will comfort them."
MATTHEW 5:4 NCV

Grief often comes out of nowhere. It's no respecter of persons. Whether that loss is a home, a job, a close friend or a family member, we've all known at one time or another what it's like to grieve.

We serve a God who is tender toward us. Even though he's majestic and powerful and has created the whole earth, he takes the time to be near us when we cry. He promises to comfort us. He's a refuge when we're going through times of trouble. He will comfort us tenderly and heal our hearts like no one else can.

Lord, thank you for your promise to comfort me when I grieve. Thank you that you are not too great to care about my sadness and that you are not too small to fix my heart.

HIDDEN IN FEAR

The LORD is my strength and my shield;
My heart trusted in Him, and I am helped;
Therefore my heart greatly rejoices,
And with my song I will praise Him.

PSALM 28:7 NKJV

Holding back from trying something new feels safe. If we don't try, we don't run the risk of failure, right? If we don't step out and be bold, we won't expose ourselves to ridicule. Bravery doesn't leave room for those excuses.

When you become a child of God, his strength is available to you. He is a shield that will protect you, far more effectively than fear or holding back ever will. If you keep holding back from trying, stretching, growing, and exploring new chances and new opportunities, your spirit will be crushed. You'll be so familiar with not going after your dreams that you won't even want to achieve them anymore.

Learn to step out in the power of God's strength. Don't stay hidden in fear any longer. Entrust your heart to God and let him be your strength.

I rejoice in your strength for me, Lord! Fear has kept me back from too much for too long. I'm ready to move toward the dreams you've given me.

GOD IS THERE

I cried out, "I am slipping!"
but your unfailing love, O LORD, supported me.
When doubts filled my mind,
your comfort gave me renewed hope and cheer.
ISAIAH 94:18-19 NLT

Life is full of ups and downs, victories and failures. Many times we feel great, and life is going well. Then there are moments when our foot slips, and we find ourselves losing balance. Sometimes we're on top of the world; other times we're ready to give up. We don't always feel strong.

It may seem like God is more present when things are going well. But even at our lowest, God is there. His love is unfailing, and it will support us through the darkest times. Don't be afraid of your own doubts. God is big enough to renew your hope and to restore your faith. He will walk with you through the darkest times and rejoice with you through the greatest.

Thank you, God, for being there for me always—when things are at their best and things are at their worst. When sadness comes over me, bring me joy. When worry takes over my mind, give me hope. When I'm happy, join me in celebrating.

JUNE

Be my rock of refuge,

to which I can always go;

give the command to save me,

for you are my rock and my fortress....

You have been my hope, Sovereign LORD,

my confidence since my youth.

PSALM 71:3, 5 NIV

TRADE REGRET FOR HOPE

"Then I will heal you of your faithlessness;
my love will know no bounds,
for my anger will be gone forever."

HOSEA 14:4 NLT

I wish. "I wish I hadn't said what I did." "I wish I had spent more time with her." "I wish I had made her feel special instead of stupid." We all can get caught up in regrets. We definitely aren't always going to get it right. We do things we regret and wish we could take back. A do-over would be really nice.

We all are tempted with sin. Though we know it's not the best choice, we go ahead anyway. After we've sinned, we feel the weight of our failure. The last thing we want to do is face God knowing that we've gone against him.

God offers us forgiveness and hope instead of regret. He promises a new chance for us. His love knows no bounds. No matter what you've done or how far you've wandered, he is ready to welcome you back with open arms. Don't be afraid or hesitant to come into his presence. He is slow to anger and overflowing in love.

God, I've stumbled. I've done things that I said I wouldn't do, and I know that I've disappointed you. Thank you for forgiving me.

THE NEW THING

"Look at the new thing I am going to do.
It is already happening. Don't you see it?
I will make a road in the desert
and rivers in the dry land."

ISAIAH 43:19 NCV

Following God might be one of the most out-of-the-ordinary things you'll do in your life. Many people won't understand why you make different choices because of your faith. Whether they, or you, realize it or not, God is doing something behind the scenes that's so much bigger than anything you could imagine.

By pressing through, God is making you stronger in your faith. Exercising the choice to do what's right even when you might be perceived as different just makes it easier to do what's right the next time around. By pressing through, you'll also be rewarded. God says that anyone who is treated badly for his sake will actually be blessed! So don't let it get to you if people aren't kind to you. God will turn it around and make it good. What he does is new and different.

God, being different isn't easy, but I know that following you is worth it. Thank you for doing something new. I can't always see what your purpose is, but I trust you enough to follow anyway.

BEING FAIR

"Treat others as you want them to treat you."

LUKE 6:31 TLB

"But that's not fair!" How many times have you heard that? How many times have you said it? No one likes to be treated unkindly, but it happens to all of us. We get hurt by someone and feel angry or frustrated. Before we know it, we've turned around and treated someone else that same way.

Treating others unfairly will never fix how we've been treated. The only way we can fight evil in this world is to do good. We have to be intentional in our relationships and stop to consider our words and our actions. That's when we'll be able to show Christ's love. By making a change in the way we treat others, our kindness will become contagious. We'll create an environment where the love of Christ is shared freely.

God, I've been treated unkindly many times and sometimes feel like taking it out on others. But you've put your love in me, and I don't want to give anything less in my relationships. Help me to be kind.

BE A LIGHT

"Let your light so shine before men, that they may see your good works and glorify your Father in heaven."

MATTHEW 5:16 NKJV

If you've ever been home at night when the lights go out, you know the first reaction is to reach for a flashlight, a candle, a match, or any sort of light. There's a lot of darkness in the world today—hate, pain, and a lot of evil— and the only thing that will chase it away is light.

Christians are called to be a light. You are called to bring hope to a hurting world. Look around you. Who in your life is surrounded by darkness? Who needs to know about God's truth and his love? Show them and tell them about the light of Jesus that gives hope. Always be ready to encourage, to comfort, to listen, to speak kindly, and to love others. Wake up each day determining in your heart to be a light to everyone you meet.

God, I want to be a light that shines your hope to the world. Many of the people in my life need you, God. I want to be the one to show and tell them that.

LET HIM IN

*"Look! I stand at the door and knock. If you hear
my voice and open the door, I will come in, and
we will share a meal together as friends."*

REVELATION 3:20 NLT

You know what is interesting about this verse? It's that
you have to open the door. Jesus will knock. He might knock
many times. But he won't come in until you've opened the
door for him. Jesus won't force his way into your heart or
your life because he wants to be welcomed in.

Jesus won't make you love him. He won't force you to
follow him. He gives you full freedom to choose. Even once
that door has been opened, closeness with the Lord means
seeking him every day. It means reading his Word, listening
to his voice, and letting him hear yours. It means allowing him
to have full say in your life. It means sharing your heart with
him. He will come knocking because he wants a relationship
with you. But you must make a choice to invite him in.

*Lord, I've heard you knocking. I've been afraid to let you in
because, although I know there's a reward, I know there's
a cost too. But I want to invite you in. Come into my heart,
Jesus. Come and be Lord of my life.*

AVOID A FIGHT

*Avoiding a fight is a mark of honor;
only fools insist on quarreling.*

PROVERBS 20:3 NLT

"Did not!"
"Did too!"
"Did not!"
"Did too!"

And round and round the arguing goes. Have you ever known someone who is always looking to pick a fight? When you enter into an argument with someone like that, it only brings you down to their level. A heated exchange is almost never productive. Instead it resolves nothing and ends up hurting everyone involved.

The best thing to do is to hold your tongue and say nothing. It takes two to fight, right? So when you don't reply to their answer with one of your own, the arguing starts to die down. Make it your goal to keep out of any foolish arguments. Staying quiet during an argument rarely makes you look stupid. Instead it will earn you respect.

God, help me not to get caught up in fights and foolish arguments. I know that in the end they will only bring harm. Help me to love people instead of fighting with them. Help me to represent you well.

LISTEN TO CORRECTION

*Whoever ignores instruction despises himself,
but he who listens to reproof gains intelligence.*
PROVERBS 15:32 ESV

Imagine if everyone viewed a red stoplight as a suggestion rather than a law. Or what if everyone ignored a warning label that something was poisonous and drank it anyway? The results wouldn't be pleasant.

These scenarios explain what this verse is about. A smart person will take the advice of someone who understands what the consequences of his actions might be. Parents correct their children because they want to keep them from the consequences they know will come if their child disobeys. A schoolteacher works hard to help students learn and understand the things that will give their students a better life. A police officer writes a ticket for a speeding driver because he or she has seen firsthand too many fatal accidents from the same carelessness. A wise person will listen to reproof and learn from it.

Lord, help me realize that people aren't trying to belittle me or insult me by giving me advice. Help me see past the way they might say it to the heart behind why they're saying it. Help me learn from their instruction, so I might live a better life.

THE NAME

*By Him let us continually offer the sacrifice of praise to God,
that is, the fruit of our lips, giving thanks to His name.*

HEBREWS 13:15 NKJV

Jesus, King of kings and Lord of lords, came to earth to
live as a man, suffered cruelty, gave his life by dying on a
cross, all to know you. It's sad when people devalue Christ's
name by using it as a swear word. When someone takes the
name of the Lord in vain, they are flippantly using a name
that is above all other names.

God created your mouth and fashioned your lips to be
able to speak, to sing, to praise. The same mouth that he
so carefully created should be speaking his name only in
thanks, in praise, in wonder. When you open your mouth to
speak the name of the Lord, check yourself first. Ask yourself
if the way you are speaking about him brings him honor or if
it disrespects him and disregards what he's done.

*Lord, forgive me for the times I've used your name
carelessly. Help me speak your name only with utmost
respect and the highest honor.*

LOVE THE UNLOVELY

"If you love those who love you, what reward do you have? Do not even the tax collectors do the same?"
MATTHEW 5:46 ESV

It's pretty easy to love the people that are popular. We're naturally drawn to people who are attractive, rich, and well-liked. On the other hand, it's difficult to go out of our comfort zones and love someone who is unpopular, uncool, and not well-off. Some people can be downright annoying or embarrassing to be seen with. Who are you trying to impress with your friendships? God? Or the people around you?

Take a moment to write down the names of five people that either upset you or are unlovely. Now make it your mission to pray for those five people every day. Then, each day, choose one name from the list and ask God to show you how to love that person in a specific, practical way. When you make a commitment to love, it won't go unnoticed. How awesome would it be to catch the eye of God!

Lord, I want to befriend those who need friends. I want to be kind to those who most people aren't kind to. Bring to my mind the people that I need to reach out to. Show me how to love like you.

BETTER THAN GOLD

How much better to get wisdom than gold,
to get insight rather than silver!
PROVERBS 16:16 NIV

It's all about the money, right? Most of us place a lot of value on being financially successful. After all, money is what gets us pretty much everything we want. We focus on our education, so we can get a good job, so we can make a good wage, so we can buy what we want.

But the Bible clearly tells us that it's more important to be wise than to be rich. You can have all the money in the world and be a fool. Money might take you all the way on this earth, but it won't take you anywhere in eternity. When you die, you can't take money with you. What matters is the life you led, the people you impacted, and the glory you gave to God. Those are the things that last into eternity!

God, help me to pursue wisdom above treasure, and insight above success. Give me eternal vision that will help me to choose based on what will last versus what will fade.

NOTHING TOO DIFFICULT

*"I am the LORD, the God of all mankind.
Is anything too hard for me?"*
JEREMIAH 32:27 NIV

Have you ever prayed to God and then thought that maybe what you were praying for was just too big of a request? God is a powerful God. Whenever you have doubts about God's ability to answer your prayer, walk out under the stars. Each pinprick of light is a planet or star that can be bigger than the earth. Your own God spoke those into existence. He keeps that planet on orbit around the sun—held in perfect balance—to keep you safe.

If you doubt God's Word or his ability to answer your prayer, you underestimate God entirely. The next time you pray, remember how awesome God really is. Remember all the miraculous things God did in the Bible. Read a story of a missionary who has seen God do something amazing. Ask a Christian you know if they've ever had a big prayer answered. You would be shocked at the stories you'd uncover. Nothing is too hard for our God.

Thank you, Lord, that even though I might doubt sometimes, you are still an all-powerful God. Teach me to trust in you. When you answer my prayer, help me to notice and to thank you for it. Help me to trust you for big things.

GUIDED BY HONESTY

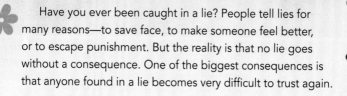

A good man is guided by his honesty;
the evil man is destroyed by his dishonesty.
PROVERBS 11:3 TLB

Have you ever been caught in a lie? People tell lies for many reasons—to save face, to make someone feel better, or to escape punishment. But the reality is that no lie goes without a consequence. One of the biggest consequences is that anyone found in a lie becomes very difficult to trust again.

Truth is always worth whatever you sacrifice to tell it. You might feel pain for a moment by exposing whatever you'd hoped to cover up, but your obedience to God won't go unrewarded. In some ways, your honesty will guide you to success because people will learn to trust you.

God, I want to be someone who is guided by honesty and not a fool who is destroyed by dishonesty. I don't want to tell lies and end up hurting those around me by my selfishness. Help me always to choose the truth.

ACCEPTABLE THOUGHTS

Let the words of my mouth and the meditation of my heart
be acceptable in your sight,
O LORD, my rock and my redeemer.
PSALM 19:14 ESV

She is so annoying! Well, that was a dumb thing for her to say! How totally lame!

How often do we get caught up with bad thoughts toward other people? We've all been hurt by people in our lives. Parents, friends and siblings aren't perfect, and it's guaranteed that they'll do things we don't like.

When we've been wronged, where do our thoughts go? If our thoughts were suddenly audible, what would people hear? That's a pretty terrifying thought. Yet this verse tells us that what we think and say should be acceptable in the sight of God. Our relationship with God should drive every aspect of our lives and cause us to always be seeking to bring him glory—even when we're irritated or angry!

Lord, would you help regulate what I'm thinking? Help me to notice when I'm giving in to resentment and bitterness or entertaining thoughts that don't please you. I want everything I think and say to be acceptable in your sight.

MEET WITH HIM

Draw near to God, and he will draw near to you.
JAMES 4:8 ESV

God is so pleased when we stop in our day to be with him. When we set time apart just to seek him, read his Word, pray, and bring him honor, he comes to meet us. He is with us throughout our day and is interested in every aspect of our lives, but when he sees us stop and look for him it brings him satisfaction.

This verse is a promise: when you come to meet the Lord, he comes to meet with you. Sometimes it might take a while to shut off all the thoughts swirling around in your head as you try to seek him. The more time you spend with him, the easier it becomes to hear him speak. Take some time today—turn on some worship music and just love him. He loves you so intensely and longs for those quiet moments with you. You are his child!

Lord, here I am. I long to feel you near me. Let me feel your precious and sweet presence. I love you so much. Help me to recognize your love and your voice.

BECOMING PERFECT

*Let patience have its perfect work, that you may
be perfect and complete, lacking nothing.*

JAMES 1:4 NKJV

Growing up is a process—and not always an easy one.
Maturity comes with a price; it's fashioned through difficulty
and learned through error. Wisdom can't be arrived at
gently; it must be earned by patience, perseverance, and
steady trust.

When trouble comes in your life, remember that it's just
another necessary hurdle in your process of maturity. You
might feel weak when you're walking through a difficult time,
but standing on the other side of it you will feel stronger
and more firmly planted than ever before. That's a promise!
Remember, you don't have to face hard things alone—
surrender your life to God and he will lead you through.

*Thank you, God, for leading me through all kinds of
difficulty and helping me toward maturity. I know that no
matter how hard all of this is, it will be worth it. Thank you
for never leaving my side. Help me to lean on you more.*

YOUR STORY

"Return to your home, and declare how much God
has done for you." So he went away, proclaiming
throughout the city how much Jesus had done for him.
LUKE 8:39 NRSV

No experience in your life is wasted. God always has something he can teach you. You may not even understand until years later why God brought you through something specific. But someday, it will all make sense.

Sometimes God will teach you things for your own growth. Other times it's not about you at all. Sometimes God will lead you through experiences or show you things so that you can impact someone's life with your story. Don't ever think that your story isn't good enough or interesting enough or happy enough or dramatic enough. Your story is your story—no one else has one just the same—and it will help someone in a way that nothing else could. Share your life story with others, encouraging them as you are able.

Heavenly Father, sometimes I don't understand why certain things happen to me. I don't know why my life looks the way that it does. But I trust that you have a unique plan for my life that couldn't be lived out by anyone else. Help me trust in your purposes.

THIS IS POSSIBLE

Jesus looked at them and said, "With man this is impossible, but with God all things are possible."
MATTHEW 19:26 NIV

Do you believe that God is able to do the impossible? We read our Bibles that Jesus did all sorts of crazy things that we can't even imagine seeing today—healing a blind man, raising a man from the dead, transforming five loaves and two fish into food for thousands. We talk all the time about how great and powerful God is, but have we seen it for ourselves?

God's power hasn't lessened, no matter how long ago those miracles happened. He is an unchanging God who is always constant. He is still doing miracles all around us—maybe we just aren't looking for them. In our age of technology and advancements, we tend to explain away almost anything with science and calculated theory. We lose our faith in exchange for rationale, and somewhere in there we've lost our miracles too. Look around you today for the miracles God is working everywhere. They are happening— you just have to have faith enough to see them.

I know, God, that you are just as powerful today as you were when Jesus walked the earth. You are capable of anything because there is no one above you. Help me to trust you for miracles and to have faith when you move.

CALL TO HIM

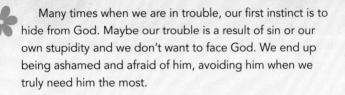

*I was in trouble, so I called to the LORD.
The LORD answered me and set me free.*

PSALM 118:5 NCV

Many times when we are in trouble, our first instinct is to hide from God. Maybe our trouble is a result of sin or our own stupidity and we don't want to face God. We end up being ashamed and afraid of him, avoiding him when we truly need him the most.

But God is our Father. He's not going to shut us out in our trouble—he wants to lift us out of it. His love for us is greater than any sin. His grace can handle whatever we might have done. When we are in trouble, instead of hiding from God, we should be calling out to him. When our life is falling apart, he will rebuild it and put it back together. When our hearts are broken, he will overwhelm us with his unconditional love. Where sin has trapped us, he will rescue us and set us free.

God, when I'm in trouble I feel afraid to come to you. I don't want you to be disappointed in me. I hate that I still sin, and I don't like causing you pain. When those times come, that's when I need you most, Lord. Set me free.

LEAVE IT BEHIND

If anyone is in Christ, he is a new creation; old things have passed away; behold, all things have become new.

2 CORINTHIANS 5:17 NKJV

God is all about new beginnings. He rewrites stories and gives hope where there's only been despair. He speaks joy into depression, he gives purpose to failure, and he makes beauty out of the ugliness in life. Whatever you've done in your life up until this point, realize that it means nothing in light of the grace of God. When you come to him in true repentance—ready for change—he will give you a new life.

If there has been darkness in your life, leave it behind. You might think, *You don't know what I've done!* but he does. And he's never stopped loving you for even a second. Refuse to remain in your past. Say goodbye to the places you've been, and put on the newness of grace and redemption.

Thank you, Jesus, for making me new. I've done things that I'm ashamed of. Things I thought made me unlovable. But you have shown me that your grace is big enough to cover the worst. Take my heart. Make me new.

LOOK FOR ME

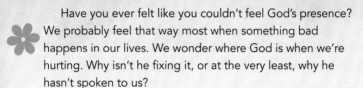

If you look for me wholeheartedly, you will find me.
JEREMIAH 29:13 NLT

Have you ever felt like you couldn't feel God's presence? We probably feel that way most when something bad happens in our lives. We wonder where God is when we're hurting. Why isn't he fixing it, or at the very least, why he hasn't spoken to us?

God doesn't hide himself from you. He wants to be found by you, to know you, to heal your heart. Go to him. Sit and wait in stillness. Read his Word and hear him speaking to you through the pages. Close your eyes, block out the noise of your life for more than a few minutes, and seek him. You will find him there. He will come to you and comfort you and heal your heart.

I need you, Jesus. I need your presence, but sometimes I feel like I can't find you. Give me the strength to look for you. Keep me always longing for you more than I want anything or anyone else.

POWER TO SAVE

*"Get rid of all moral filth and the evil that is
so prevalent and humbly accept the word
planted in you, which can save you."*

Luke 10:27 NIV

What we put into our minds has power over us. Every movie, video game, and what books we read have an effect. When we are taking in things that are evil—or not honoring to God—we destroy our minds and our heart. That sounds extreme because it really feels harmless. What happens subtly below the surface isn't harmless. We are slowly, but deeply, being affected by everything we take in.

When we focus on things that are filled with God's truth and that bring messages of purity, life, and light, then our minds are being built up. We are becoming better from what we are hearing and seeing. The fruit of that will come out in our lives. When God convicts you to look away from something—listen to him.

God, help me to be more in tune with what is good and what is bad for my mind. I want to be wise about what I take in because I know that it will influence what comes out.

GREATER LOVE

*"Greater love has no one than this, that
one lay down his life for his friends."*

JOHN 15:13 NASB

We all want to be loved. We look for love in a million
places. Whether we realize it or not, we are on a hunt to
be loved. We look to be loved by parents, siblings, friends,
a boyfriend, even through social media. But while those
people can and probably do love you, no one will ever love
you the way that God does. The depth of his love for you is
unmatched.

God loves you unconditionally. He won't love you any
less if you ignore him or are angry with him. You'll definitely
hurt him by doing those things, but he is faithful and his love
is true. When you stop and think for even a moment about
how incredible and different this type of love is, you can't
help but feel love for him in return. The more you spend
time in his presence, the more you will be able to really feel
the love that's been there all along.

*God, thank you for a love that's unlike any other. Thank
you for being constant when nothing else is. Thank you for
loving me even when I'm not the most loving toward you.*

COMPLIMENTS

Each of us should please our neighbors
for their good, to build them up.

ROMANS 15:2 NIV

"I really like your new shoes." "Your hair looks so nice."
"You have a beautiful smile!" Complimenting someone is so
simple. It could be the best part of someone's day. Maybe
by telling someone that her hair looks nice, you made her
feel beautiful. Maybe by complimenting her on her smile,
you reminded her that it's ok to feel happy, despite the
deep sadness in her life.

Kindness costs nothing, and might actually be worth
everything to the one you are kind to. Make it your mission
today to be kind and encouraging to everyone you meet.
Choose one thing about each person you meet that is
noteworthy. Then share it with him or her—out loud. Not
only will you bring joy to everyone you encourage, but you
will feel good doing it.

God, help me look for the best in others and then to call it
out in them. I want to be an encouragement wherever I go.
I want to bring your joy, your light, and your love with me
everywhere.

COMPARING

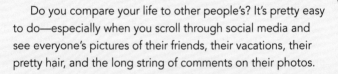

Oh, don't worry; we wouldn't dare say that we are as wonderful as these other men who tell you how important they are! But they are only comparing themselves with each other, using themselves as the standard of measurement. How ignorant!

2 CORINTHIANS 10:12 NLT

Do you compare your life to other people's? It's pretty easy to do—especially when you scroll through social media and see everyone's pictures of their friends, their vacations, their pretty hair, and the long string of comments on their photos.

Whether or not life looks good on your Instagram profile doesn't matter much in the grand scheme of things. When you look on social media, you're only seeing highlights of what's really going on in someone else's world. No matter how perfect their pictures look or how many followers they have, they still have the same ups and downs in life that you have. They deal with the same insecurities and have many of the same imperfections. Don't fall into the cycle of comparing yourself with others. It will only make you dissatisfied.

Jesus, teach me to be thankful for the life I have instead of wanting the life someone else has. You have created me to be who I am, where I live, with the body have. I praise you for how you've chosen to make me.

THE SAME

Jesus Christ is the same yesterday, today, and forever.
HEBREWS 13:8 NKJV

Have you ever felt frustrated with people who change their mind over and over again? Or change entire things about their personality? One day we think we have someone figured out, and the next we are blindsided by something they do or say. People can be pretty unreliable.

There is one person in our lives who we can count on to never change. Not even a bit. Jesus is the same today as he's always been. When you read about him in the Bible, and the things he said and did, he'd do those same things if he showed up in your town. He will never change. He is who he is and nothing will change him. You can trust that when he says something to you, it will always be true.

Thank you, Jesus, that I can trust you. I don't have to wonder if you'll change, if you'll stop loving me tomorrow, or if the words I read in the Bible won't be true in ten or even a hundred years. I can trust in you—completely.

THE WORD GIVES LIGHT

The unfolding of your words gives light;
it gives understanding to the simple.
PSALM 119:130 NIV

The Bible might seem daunting sometimes. It's a thick book full of small words and concepts that seem hard to understand. The thing about the Bible is that the more you read it, the more you understand. You're growing and learning as you read the words in it. By faithfully reading the words of truth, even when you don't fully feel like you're understanding what's being said, its truths are being written on your heart and sealed in your soul.

Be faithful in reading the Word, and you'll find your entire life begins to change. In every situation, the words of truth will come to your mind and guide your reactions. You will become more peaceful, more joyful, more faithful, and more wise. People will begin to come to you for advice because they will recognize that there is a light and a knowledge in you that is uncommon.

God, I struggle with regularly reading your Word. Help me to hunger for it. I want to be so full of your truth that it comes out naturally whenever I open my mouth to speak. I want your words to flow through me instead of my own.

POSITION OF AUTHORITY

Everyone must submit to governing authorities. For all authority comes from God, and those in positions of authority have been placed there by God.

ROMANS 13:1 NLT

None of us like being told what to do. We want to be in charge of ourselves—free to decide what we do and how we do it. It seems like there is a natural desire inside us to rebel against authority.

Submitting ourselves to human leadership trains our hearts to submit to God. Do you want to be used by God? God can't use someone that isn't willing to obey him without question. Do you want to live a life that's led by his Spirit and rewarded with his blessing? Then practice now by obeying the leaders that God has put in your life. Your parents, teachers, youth pastor, mentors—they have been put in your life for a specific reason. You will miss out on some incredible relationships and some very valuable wisdom if you resist their leadership.

Dear heavenly Father, you know that it's not always easy for me to obey the people in authority over me. Please help me to humble myself and to trust those you've placed over me.

I STILL HAVE YOU

I was naked when I was born, and I will be naked when I die.
The LORD gave these things to me,
and he has taken them away.
Praise the name of the LORD.

JOB 1:21 NCV

When Job said this, he had just lost everything he owned, and his children had been killed. Job had gone from extreme wealth and success to complete loss and poverty. During this time, Job realized something very important. Even with everything that he'd lost, he still had what was most important—God.

We all love stuff. God. If everything we owned was taken away from us, would we get angry and complain? Or would we worship God regardless? You may have experienced a significant loss in your life that left you feeling hurt and angry. If you continue to read the story of Job, you will learn that God was very near to Job. He cared for Job. If you have gone through a time of trial, remember to call out to God. Purpose in your heart to praise him no matter what happens. He will be there for you.

Father, I want to stop and thank you for the things that you have blessed me with. Help me remember it is you who allows me to have the things I have. Thank you that no matter what happens I still have you. Even if I lose everything, I will still have you.

GOOD GIFTS

*Every good and perfect gift is from above, coming
down from the Father of the heavenly lights,
who does not change like shifting shadows.*

JAMES 1:17 NIV

When God created you he gave you a personality. He
knew what you would enjoy and what would make you
happy. When God created the Garden of Eden, he gave
man and woman authority over that garden. It was a gift—a
place handmade by their Creator for them to enjoy. He
created their ability to laugh, to sing, to feel love, joy, and
excitement. God gives us perfect gifts.

Take a moment and make a list of ten things God has
given you. What do you find beautiful? Have you watched
the sunrise and been amazed by the colors dancing across
the sky? Have you held a snowflake in your hand and
marveled at its intricacies? Have you felt the warm sun on
your back on a bright summer day? Remember each of
those moments and thank God for them. They are gifts from
God! He loves you immeasurably, and his kindness to you is
shown in these things.

*Father, help me to notice the little things and to be thankful
for them. The next time I am enjoying something that you
have created, remind me that it was made for my pleasure.*

HOW TO TREAT OTHERS

Do nothing from selfish ambition or conceit, but in humility count others more significant than yourselves.
PHILIPPIANS 2:3 ESV

This statement can be hard one to swallow. What does it mean to think others are more significant than we are? We naturally look out for our own interests. We get hungry, we feed ourselves; we get thirsty, we grab a drink; we are bored, we turn on the TV.

What this verse is saying is that before you meet your own needs, you should be looking to meet the needs of others. Pretend there's only one piece of pizza left, and you're still hungry. The natural first instinct is to grab the piece and eat it. What this verse says is that you might offer that slice of pizza to your friend before grabbing it for yourself. This might be a silly example, but it has big implications. Treat others more highly than you treat yourself.

God, help me to notice the needs of others. I don't want to be so focused on my own desires that I miss out on a chance to help someone else.

JULY

This is the confidence that we have
toward him, that if we ask anything
according to his will he hears us.
And if we know that he hears us
in whatever we ask, we know that we have the
requests that we have asked of him.

1 John 5:14–15 esv

WORKING FOR GOD

Whatever you do, work at it with all your heart, as working for the Lord, not for human masters, since you know that you will receive an inheritance from the Lord as a reward. It is the Lord Christ you are serving.

COLOSSIANS 3:23-24 NIV

We all have those moments when we feel like our job is awful or that school is boring and pointless. But if we stop and consider this verse, we learn that it is important to treat our work and school as if we were there for God. Work harder than the person next to you. Strive to excel in everything. Dance class? Give it all you've got. Sports? Hit it hard—be the best you can be. After-school job? Go the extra mile and do more than what is expected of you.

The next time that you're feeling underappreciated, bored, or tired of your work—use those feelings as motivation to work even harder. Remember that as a Christian, the world is constantly examining you to see what kind of person you really are.

Lord, help me remember that I am your representative. I want people to speak well of me because I serve you. I really want others to know that I work hard and strive for excellence because I know that I am doing it for you.

DO GOOD

*Do not forget to do good and to share, for
with such sacrifices God is well pleased.*

HEBREWS 13:16 NKJV

God loves the poor. Throughout Scripture he says to
think about the needs of others and to help them. When
was the last time you looked around you and paid attention
to what other people didn't have? When we take time to
help others who have genuine needs, it pleases the Lord.
What better thing could you possibly do than please the
Lord? If you love him, do the things he loves.

Take a moment and ask God to show you ways that you
can give to people who don't have much. Ask your family
if they have ideas so you can do it together. If one of your
friends doesn't have a lot of food for lunch, could you
share with them and meet their need that way? If someone
doesn't have a ride home from school, could you offer them
one? When God sees you helping those who have less than
you do, he is pleased with you!

*Help me to notice people in need and to know how to
help meet their needs. I want to please you by giving the
blessings that I have been given to those who really need it.*

REJOICE IN THIS DAY

This is the day that the LORD has made;
let us rejoice and be glad in it.
PSALM 118:24 NRSV

Today, this day, is a gift from God. Think back in your life for a moment. What were you doing two hundred years ago? Can you remember? Absolutely nothing. You had never seen the sun, you'd never known love or friendship, you'd never breathed in the winter air, you'd never laughed. You didn't know about any of these things because you didn't exist.

You aren't guaranteed any more days, either. No one is promised a tomorrow. Your life is precious, and every single day is a gift from God. Rejoice and be glad that God has made and given you this day. Take time right now and thank him for it. Then go out, and make the most of the day you've been given.

Lord, I don't know what today will bring, but one thing I
do know is that I am thankful for it. You have given me a
wonderful gift by giving me today. Thank you for creating
me. You didn't have to make me, and yet you did. I will
rejoice in this day.

FREEDOM IN TRUTH

"You shall know the truth, and the truth shall make you free."

JOHN 8:32 NKJV

Have you ever felt like you were stuck in one spot inside your own head but then had a moment of clarity that completely changed everything? Many times we begin to believe a lie that we heard from someone else. We allow that lie to keep us trapped inside a box we've created in our own minds. We find our identity in a lie that holds us back.

God's Word is truth and acts as a key to your self-created boxes. His Word sets you free from the limits lies have placed on you. When you read the Scripture and find words of truth, they have the power to set you free from years of bondage. Reading the Bible is so important because it brings healing to what's broken in your life. God's truth will set you free and help you become the person he longs for you to be.

Lord, when I open your Word, bring me to the verses that will set me free from lies that have held me back. I do want you to work in my life. I will open your Word and my heart so that you can do your work in me.

ABLE TO SAVE

He is able always to save those who come to God through
him because he always lives, asking God to help them.
HEBREWS 7:25 NCV

Have you ever wondered if you were beyond saving?
Maybe you've done something that feels so terrible or
so against God's plan for your life that you doubt he can
forgive you. Or maybe you haven't wondered that about
yourself, but you've judged other people in your life and
thought that surely they couldn't be accepted by God.

Jesus is able to save anyone—absolutely anyone. As long
as they come to God through Jesus Christ, he will offer them
salvation. Jesus stands up for each person, always ready to
plead their case to the Father. God is a God of justice, but
he offers grace to the humble. If you've done something that
feels unforgivable, come and ask God for mercy. And don't
judge anyone else, determining that they can't receive his
grace. No one is too far-gone for him to reach.

God, your grace is so powerful that I can't comprehend it.
When I think I've done too much, you tell me that you still
love me anyway. I don't deserve your love, but I'm thankful
for it.

LOVE WITH ACTION

If someone says, "I love God," and hates his brother, he is a liar; for the one who does not love his brother whom he has seen, cannot love God whom he has not seen.

1 JOHN 4:20 NASB

You can say you love someone, but how much does that really mean if you don't show it? Love without action is nothing. God is love. Not love for those who love him back, or those who are easy to love—just simple, no-strings-attached love.

You can say that you love God, but if you aren't expressing that by loving the people he created, then it means nothing. If you want to love God well, then act it out by loving his people. Loving means setting aside your own needs for someone else. It means being kind, even when you don't feel like it. It means helping someone when you just want to look out for yourself. It means being patient when you've already lost your temper. If you can't love the people around you, then how can you truly love God who is so much less tangible to you? Practice living a life of love with action.

Help me to love everyone, Lord. Give me your heart for everyone around me.

THE LIST

Those who lead blameless lives and do what is right,
speaking the truth from sincere hearts.
Those who refuse to gossip
or harm their neighbors
or speak evil of their friends.

PSALM 15:2-3 NLT

This passage describes the person who is allowed to go into God's presence. Read the list again. Do you feel like you fit that description? Those are pretty high standards. But God created you for life of the highest standard because he wants his people to glorify him by purity, kindness, and love.

Take this list and make it your credo. Try to live by its rules. You'll fail—that's guaranteed. And it's okay because the blood of Jesus covers your failures. But do your best to stay away from what you know to be wrong. Speak the truth. Don't do anything to hurt the people you know. Don't talk about others behind their backs. All of these will not only bring glory to God when you do them, but they also will just make you a better friend, child, sibling, and person.

Thank you, Lord, for setting out these guidelines that brings honor to you. I want to be someone who my friends can trust, my parents can be proud of, and you can delight in.

LIVING IN PURITY

How can a young person live a pure life?
By obeying your word.
PSALM 119:9 NCV

It can seem pretty impossible to live a pure life. There is so much impurity around us, and all too often the lines get blurred between right and wrong. The reality is there's no way to measure purity except by the Word of God. So much has gotten twisted by our own perceptions, culture, and what the world tells us is ok. Staying pure doesn't even seem important anymore. When so many people around us aren't living in purity, it seems pointless to be different. But by honoring God's plan for us—physically, visually, and mentally—we will be rewarded.

Don't think that you're saying no for nothing. You are laying the foundation for a healthy life and a healthy relationship with the Lord. Don't pile up regret for yourself. Live your life and hold your head high, knowing you've pleased and obeyed God.

God, it's not easy to stay pure, especially when none of my friends are. I know that you give good things. I know that if I do things your way, I'll be reaping the benefit for years to come.

UNSELFISH & CONSIDERATE

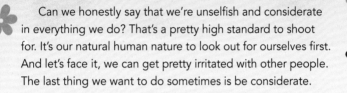

Let everyone see that you are unselfish and considerate
in all you do. Remember that the Lord is coming soon.

PHILIPPIANS 4:5 TLB

Can we honestly say that we're unselfish and considerate
in everything we do? That's a pretty high standard to shoot
for. It's our natural human nature to look out for ourselves first.
And let's face it, we can get pretty irritated with other people.
The last thing we want to do sometimes is be considerate.

God is reminding us of something in this verse—Jesus is
coming back soon. Our little annoyances or preferences matter
little in light of the grander scheme of eternity. No matter
how justified we feel in treating someone less than best, what
matters most is how we prepare the way for the coming of the
Lord. Are we living out the purposes of Christ on the earth? Or
are we just seeking ways to elevate ourselves?

Question your motives and ask God for help to live your
best life for him.

God, I want to be ready for your coming. Help me to live a
life that will bring you honor and prepare the way for you to
come back.

STAND IN FAITH

He must ask in faith without any doubting,
for the one who doubts is like the surf of the
sea, driven and tossed by the wind.

JAMES 1:6 NASB

We're taught to question everything: don't take anything at face value, do your research, don't set yourself up for disappointment, use healthy skepticism. Each of these principles has a point, but when you come to God in faith—asking him to do something—you can't question him. Imagine asking God to take away your fear. You must ask him for that with total confidence that he will do it. If you ask, and then step back and start to worry and think about your back-up plan if God doesn't come through, then you'll have nothing to stand on.

God has promised that there's no fear in love. He has promised to save you. If you don't buy into those promises, then what do you have? You have to determine in your heart that you're going to believe what he says. If you don't do that, you'll be just like the surface of a raging ocean—never still, never calm, never resolved. Ask him in faith, and then continue in faith as you wait.

God, give me complete confidence in your ability to answer my prayers. Help me to stand in faith.

203

REALITY OF ETERNAL LIFE

I write these things to you who believe in the name of the Son of God, so that you may know that you have eternal life.

1 JOHN 5:13 NRSV

Do you know that you have eternal life? Are you confident in the salvation of Jesus? When you think about death, are you certain of what awaits you on the other side? It might feel morbid to talk about, but what's being said in this verse is anything but dark. The writer was trying to connect these people to the reality that they have eternal life! The greatest reward imaginable is theirs already.

If you've believed in the name of Jesus Christ and acknowledged his power to save you, then you're in. If you rely on his grace and his mercy and his forgiveness, you'll live forever. These aren't nice ideas or comforting stories. This is truth. If you believe in Jesus, then you need to know—really know—that you have eternal life with him. Take a few minutes and absorb that reality. Think on it long enough that it becomes as real as the breath in your lungs. Once you feel you've grasped the truth of it, thank God.

Lord, I'm awestruck by the reality of the eternal life that waits for me. Thank you for allowing me to be forgiven of all that I've done wrong. I can't wait to see you face to face.

ENJOYING RULES

*I enjoy living by your rules
as people enjoy great riches.*
PSALM 119:14 NCV

It feels a little odd to be talking about liking rules. Our natural response to rules is normally something closer to frustration than enjoyment. The psalmist recognized the rich benefits of obedience in his life. He realized that by obeying the Lord, he would actually live a better life. A life that was as enjoyable as luxury is to a rich person.

The human heart is easily deceived. We're tempted to be sidetracked in a million directions by pursuing all kinds of things. By staying within the guidelines and rules set out by God in his Word, we can trust that our hearts are being led in the best possible direction. Our own simple act of obedience will lead to a life of fulfillment and wealth in him.

God, I give my heart to you. I commit to following your boundaries for my life. Help me to learn to enjoy obedience. Give me an excitement to follow your rules and to recognize my own richness in your plan.

OUR FIGHT

Our fight is not against people on earth but against the rulers and authorities and the powers of this world's darkness, against the spiritual powers of evil in the heavenly world.

EPHESIANS 6:12 NCV

It's easy to think that what we can't see doesn't exist. The concept of angels and demons can sound eerie and almost fantastical to us. In our minds, we have cartoon characters or media images connected with those beings, and to a point, it removes their reality. There *is* a spiritual realm that truly exists; it's real and it's not to be messed with.

There is a war going on in the heavenly realm. Be careful how you engage in this battle. Be aware of what you let into your mind and heart. Remember also that God is more powerful than any other being in this universe. You don't have to fear the powers of darkness, but you must be aware. Call on the name of Jesus and claim his power over your life. He is more than able to keep you safe and to fight your battles.

God, I admit that I don't think often enough about the spiritual battle going on. Thank you for your power on my life. I know that I don't have to fear the darkness. Help me to stay alert. Don't let me be pulled in by things that aren't of you.

YOU LOVED THEM

It wasn't their swords that took the land.
It wasn't their power that gave them victory.
But it was your great power and strength.
You were with them because you loved them.

PSALM 44:3 NCV

Do you ever feel powerless? Like you're trapped in your own life, unable to fix what's broken? You know you can't save yourself; you just aren't armed for it. Life can be hard. There are so many things that will come at you from a million directions and make you feel defenseless. Drama with friends, trouble with parents, mistakes you've made that you don't know how to fix.

Don't lose heart. You are not left alone to fight your battles. You have a God who loves you enough to fight for you. He is powerful and strong. And he is compelled by his love for you. Beloved, he died for you. What makes you think he wouldn't be willing to put himself into your fight and win it for you? You are his child, and he loves you.

Thank you, God, that you are here to fight my battles. I need your strength in my life. I feel powerless to save myself and know I'll never be able to. You are with me because you love me, and that makes all the difference.

NOT ONE FORGOTTEN

"Are not five sparrows sold for two pennies? Yet not one of them is forgotten in God's sight. But even the hairs of your head are all counted. Do not be afraid; you are of more value than many sparrows."

LUKE 12:6-7 NRSV

In a world of over seven billion people, it's easy to feel like just one insignificant face in the crowd. We wonder if God really cares about our lives and our thoughts and our heartbreaks. How could he with so many people to keep track of?

But if even the sparrow—who is such a small and seemingly insignificant animal—isn't forgotten or overlooked by God, how much more likely is he to know you and your heart? You are a human being, created in the image of God with a soul, mind, and will that are known by him. He's not far removed. He's not high above, looking down at you from a distance. He is with you. He knows the thoughts and the dreams of your heart even better than you do. Trust that his love for you is as intimate as it is vast.

Thank you, God, for including this verse in the Bible. You knew that in my insecurity, I might wonder if I mattered much to you. You took the time to reassure me that I do.

MULTIPLIED WORRY

When anxiety was great within me
your consolation brought me joy.

PSALM 94:19 NIV

There always seems to be something to worry about. Our life is full of unknowns, and it's only natural to wonder about what we can't predict. We become anxious about everything from what we'll wear, to an important event, to what we'll do in life. And it always seems like one worry leads to another—they multiply each another.

When we begin to become overwhelmed by our own anxiety, God's peace can calm our fears. If we open the Bible, we'll be bombarded with truths that dissolve our worries. So many of the things we were anxious about will literally disappear when we shine the light of God's truth on them. The foolishness of our fear is exposed when we recognize that God is ultimately in control—no matter what possibilities exist.

Thank you, God, that you are a safe place for my wondering heart. I get scared about the future and about the details of my life, but your Word is full of truths that remind me that you're bigger than my worry.

DO WHAT IT SAYS

Don't just listen to God's word. You must do what it says. Otherwise, you are only fooling yourselves.
JAMES 1:22 NLT

It's not enough just to go to church or youth group and hear the Word of God. It's not enough to read your Bible or your devotional for the day and then walk away. If you aren't actually taking what you've read and applying it to your life, then what good has it really done you?

You can sit and watch drawing tutorials all day long, watching techniques and learning terms. Will that be enough to make you a great artist even though you've never drawn a single thing? No, of course not. Not if you've never put pen to paper. It's the same with the Word of God. You can read all day long about how to live a good life, but if you don't practice what it says, your life won't be changed.

God, help me to apply your Word to my life. I don't want to fool myself into thinking that I'm living according to your plan, when in reality I'm just filling my mind with knowledge without leading a life to match.

ALL GOD HAS

"Things which eye has not seen and ear has not heard,
And which have not entered the heart of man,
All that God has prepared for those who love Him."
1 CORINTHIANS 2:9 NASB

What God has for us is so much better than what we could dream up for ourselves. We think we know what's best for us. We think we know what would make us happy. If a certain someone loved us back, then we'd be happy. If we had success, fame, money, then we'd be happy.

The reality is that God created you—mind, body, and soul. He knows the inner workings of your heart, and he knows how to bring you true joy that won't ever fade. What he has in store for you will blow your mind. Don't spend your life desiring what you'll never have. Love God, invest in your relationship with him, and trust him to make you happy. The rewards that he will give are better than any reward the world could offer.

God, help me to trust that you desire for me to be happy. I don't want to look at your gifts as second best, because I know they aren't. You created me—I don't have to be afraid that you won't give what's best for me.

UNLESS THE LORD

Unless the Lord builds the house,
the builders labor in vain.
Unless the Lord watches over the city,
the guards stand watch in vain.

Psalm 127:1 niv

Don't try to fight for something that God isn't in. Sometimes it's tempting to start something, and then ask God to bless it after the fact. But did he really want you to start it? For example, if you get into a relationship with someone without seeking God, you need to find out if that relationship is God's will for you *before* you ask him to bless it.

Seek the face of the Lord continually. He will speak into your life and he will guide and direct you if you have opened your heart to him. When you are walking in continual communication with God, your life will reflect his blessing and his peace. Only he knows the end from the beginning—so why wouldn't you trust your life to him?

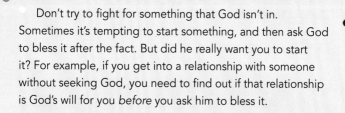

God, I don't want to build something in my life that you're not a part of. I don't want to start something if your blessing isn't on it. Guide me in all things so that I can put myself fully into the things that you've ordained.

THINK ABOUT GOD

*Set your minds on things that are above,
not on things that are on earth.*

COLOSSIANS 3:2 NRSV

When you let your mind dwell on Jesus, his Word, his life, and what he's done for you—then you won't be able to stop thinking about him. His greatness is mysterious. His love is beyond comprehension. He's fascinating!

But the things of the world are pretty good at pushing his holiness out of our minds. Sin can also be fascinating. The difference between the two is that one leads to life and the other to death. When we consciously choose to fill our minds with the things of God, we are investing in our own lives in eternity. But when we push away the voice of conviction, we are allowing death to reign in our minds. We are pushing God out of the place that he belongs. Think carefully about what you're thinking about.

Jesus, be first in my thoughts. When thoughts come that aren't of you, give me the strength to push them out. Help me to be more and more fascinated by you so that you are the subject of my thoughts and my dreams.

GIVE ME YOUR HEART

Give me your heart.
May your eyes take delight in following my ways.
PROVERBS 23:26 NLT

Our hearts are easily persuaded. We might be so sure of something in our heads, but if our hearts leads us elsewhere, we're almost left defenseless. It's hard to know how to trust our hearts. You're told constantly to follow your heart, but that can be hard when it pulls you in different directions.

That's why God says to give him your heart. He created that heart of yours, and he loves you. He doesn't want to see you heartbroken or disappointed. He wants to see you happy—living your best possible life. Following your heart alone can lead you places that you never wanted to go. But when you give your heart to God and then you follow him, you can trust that your happiness is in the best of hands.

Lord, I give you my heart. Take it and lead me wherever you want me to go. I don't want to spend these years of my life being heartbroken. I want to let you lead me to happiness because I know that the joy you give is everlasting.

HAVE NOTHING TO DO

*Have nothing to do with the fruitless deeds of
darkness, but rather expose them. It is shameful even
to mention what the disobedient do in secret.*
EPHESIANS 5:11-12 NIV

Have you ever had a friend ask you to cover for them?
You're torn between wanting to help and knowing that what
they're doing is not the best thing for them. What harm
could come from keeping your mouth shut or telling a small
lie for them? After all, you're not the one doing it.

By hiding someone's sin, you're actually participating in
it. The Word tells us that we need to expose the worthless
things that are done in secret. If it's shameful to even
mention it, then how much more shameful is it for you to
make it possible for the sin to happen? Wash your hands
of these kinds of situations. Choose never to be involved—
even in a small way.

*God, give me the strength not to be involved in sin in any
capacity. When someone asks me to be part of what they're
doing wrong, I ask that you would give me the strength to resist.*

A POWERFUL FORCE

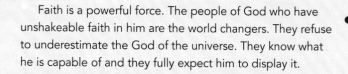

"Truly I tell you, if you say to this mountain, 'Be taken up and thrown into the sea,' and if you do not doubt in your heart, but believe that what you say will come to pass, it will be done for you."

MARK 11:23 NRSV

Faith is a powerful force. The people of God who have unshakeable faith in him are the world changers. They refuse to underestimate the God of the universe. They know what he is capable of and they fully expect him to display it.

How strong is your faith? Do you believe that God could heal you of sickness? Do you believe that he could make you walk on water? If you are a natural skeptic, then take a few minutes and ask God to show you a display of his power in your life. Then ask him to give you insight regarding it. Ask in boldness—and believe that he can and will answer you.

God, I know that you are powerful. Sometimes I forget to look for your power on display. I know that you are working miracles all around me, every day. Help me to see them. Give me the faith to believe that I will.

ENEMIES AT PEACE

When people's lives please the LORD,
even their enemies are at peace with them.

PROVERBS 16:7 NLT

When you live in a way that's pleasing to God, it means you're leading a life marked by love, forgiveness, grace, and kindness. When people see you living that way, they can't find a bad thing to say about you. You've shown so much grace and love to others, what can they say against you? Even people that you've been at odds with in the past will feel their anger neutralized by your love.

Do your best to live according to the Word of God. Be someone who shares Christ's love just by the way you live. Maybe in the past you've had enemies. You've had people who didn't like you and didn't treat you well. But if you start to treat them in a way that is godly, their anger won't be able to stand. Conduct yourself with kindness. Act in patience. Offer mercy. Love above all else.

Thank you, God, that you've given me a way to live at peace with even my enemies. I want to lead a life that pleases you. Thank you for giving me all the tools to do that.

PUTTING ON THE BRAKES

A person without self-control
is like a city with broken-down walls.
PROVERBS 25:28 NLT

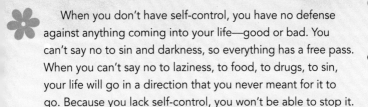

When you don't have self-control, you have no defense against anything coming into your life—good or bad. You can't say no to sin and darkness, so everything has a free pass. When you can't say no to laziness, to food, to drugs, to sin, your life will go in a direction that you never meant for it to go. Because you lack self-control, you won't be able to stop it.

Imagine that you're in a car, going down a steep hill toward the ocean. Self-control is like the brakes. Without them, you'll just keep flying forward, hurtling in a direction that will eventually lead to tragedy. By applying a little bit of self-control, you'll slow to a speed where you can see ahead of you and turn away when it's time. Ask God to help you learn self-control. When something is about to harm you, you can put on the brakes and stop giving it entrance into your life.

God give me more self-control. I am easily led down a path of overindulgence. I say yes to too many things. When I know something is bad for me, help me put the brakes on.

A THOUSAND GENERATIONS

Know therefore that the LORD your God is God;
he is the faithful God, keeping his covenant of
love to a thousand generations of those who
love him and keep his commandments.

DEUTERONOMY 7:9 NIV

Do you ever think that the promises in the Bible weren't meant for you? Like only David could fight a giant with God's power. Or only Jonah could run from God and still have God love and redeem him. Or only Esther could be given a bravery that was supernatural.

God says outright in this verse that his love is a promise he made for a thousand generations. Beloved, that clearly includes you. His love, his promises, his miracles, and his power are for you. When he promised Abraham a legacy of glory, he was including you in that. When he promised the disciples as he left the earth that he would return for them, he meant for you too.

God, it's powerful to realize that your love and your
promises are for me. They'll never run out. Help me to read
your Word with the perspective that all of this is for me. I
want to walk in the confidence of that truth.

WEIGHT OF CRITICISM

Do not let anyone treat you as if you are unimportant
because you are young. Instead, be an example
to the believers with your words, your actions,
your love, your faith, and your pure life.

1 TIMOTHY 4:12 NCV

Words can go a long way in your mind. They can either build you up, or they can crush your spirit. When you face a lot of negativity about anything, it's easy to want to give up. You don't feel strong enough to stand under the weight of criticism. Proving yourself sounds appealing, but far too difficult.

When Paul wrote these words to Timothy, he knew that Timothy would've faced some criticism for his age. Timothy was a pretty young guy who was put in a place of authority. Naturally, some people might have felt threatened by that. When people feel challenged or threatened, they can speak out in criticism.

If you're put in a position like Timothy was—where you're being criticized for something God told you to do—then extend grace to those in opposition. But continue doing the Lord's will. It will be worth it when you press through.

Lord, help me to focus on what you say about me over what others do.

PEACE OR ENVY

A heart at peace gives life to the body,
but envy rots the bones.
PROVERBS 14:30 NIV

It's interesting that in this verse, envy is listed as the opposite of peace. Normally we would say "war" is the opposite of peace. But when you become jealous of someone, you lose your contentment with yourself. And you can't remain at peace if you're at odds with your life. When you focus on something that you don't have, it's impossible to feel the calm that can comes with satisfaction. As you continue to want what others have, you lose joy in what is already yours.

By choosing to remain thankful and content with what you have, you choose to enjoy life to the fullest. As long as you're comparing what you have to someone else and growing in jealousy, you'll be unhappy. Choose today to be happy with who you are and what you have.

Thank you, Lord, for everything you've given me. I do
struggle with wanting things I don't have, but you created
me to be content with the life I've been given. I can find full
joy in the life I live now because of you.

THIS IS THE WAY

When you turn to the right or when you turn to the left, your ears shall hear a word behind you, saying, "This is the way; walk in it."

ISAIAH 30:21 NRSV

We worry a lot about missing God's will. We are already convinced that his will is best for us—but what does that mean if we can't find what his will is? Especially as we start thinking about college and beyond, it's easier to stress about making the right choice. How can we be sure that what we are choosing is his choice for our lives?

The beautiful part about being a child of God is that we are given the Holy Spirit who leads us into all truth. God promises that no matter what direction we need in life, we will hear his voice speaking to us and telling us where to go. We'll know in our spirits what he has in store for us. Continue to practice hearing him through prayer and study of his Word. He'll lead you on the best path.

God, I want to live your plan for my life because I know it's the best plan. Sometimes I worry that I'll miss out on what you want for me, but I know that you don't want to hide your will from me. I know that you are speaking to me. Help me to listen.

SAFER IN HIS HANDS

When I am afraid, I will put my trust in You.
In God, whose word I praise,
In God I have put my trust; I shall not be afraid.
What can mere man do to me?

PSALM 56:3-4 NASB

Trust isn't easy. Trust means letting go. It means giving up control. Trust means believing that someone else can handle something as well or better than we can. Trust isn't usually our first reaction. Typically we want to hold on to the things that are valuable to us as tightly as we can—letting go of them is the last thing we want.

There is one person we can trust with everything we have. One person who can always handle it better than we can. God is trustworthy. He's never shown himself to be anything less. You can trust him with whatever situation comes your way. And you can trust him with your whole life. When fear overtakes you and you want to take back control, remember that your life is far safer in his hands than it would ever be in yours.

Lord, I know that you are trustworthy. When it comes to actually placing my life in your hands, I get fearful. Give me peace and the knowledge that you are to be trusted completely. You've never let me down, and I know that you never will.

NOT EMBARRASSED

I am not ashamed of the gospel, because it is the power of God that brings salvation to everyone who believes: first to the Jew, then to the Gentile.

ROMANS 1:16 NIV

Do you ever feel embarrassed by your faith? Christians don't always get the best rap. Unfortunately, a lot of people in the world see us as being judgmental, self-righteous, and obnoxious. When we tell someone we're Christians, we instantly have to fight with that stereotype.

If we truly believe that what we have in Jesus is the answer to everything wrong in the world, then we'll shout it from the rooftops. We won't care what anyone thinks. If a tidal wave were about to sweep over your school, would you keep quiet because people might think you're crazy? No! You'd run around telling everyone! You wouldn't want anyone to die because you were too scared to say something. Stop worrying about what people will think of you. Give them the best news they'll ever hear.

Jesus I want to be a life changer. I want to bring the news of your power and salvation to everyone I meet. Give me boldness.

AUGUST

May he give you the power
to accomplish all the good things
your faith prompts you to do.

2 THESSALONIANS 1:11 NLT

TURN BACK THE CLOCK

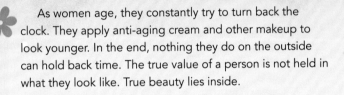

Charm is deceitful and beauty is passing,
But a woman who fears the LORD, she shall be praised.
PROVERBS 31:30 NKJV

As women age, they constantly try to turn back the clock. They apply anti-aging cream and other makeup to look younger. In the end, nothing they do on the outside can hold back time. The true value of a person is not held in what they look like. True beauty lies inside.

A woman that loves God will be forgiving, caring, compassionate, and full of love because she has the vibrant presence of God within her. Women who are committed to the Lord will emanate an inner beauty that amplifies their outer beauty.

Lord, you see what's inside of me. Change me from the inside out. I know that my outer beauty will fade, but my inner beauty can continue to grow as I become more like you.

CHOOSE WISELY

Whoever walks with the wise becomes wise,
but the companion of fools will suffer harm.
PROVERBS 13:20 ESV

It's important to choose your friends wisely. If you choose a group of people who are always talking about sex, drugs, and other things they've done wrong, you'll eventually get caught up in their lifestyle—or at least brought down by it. On the other hand, if you choose a group of Christian friends who have set standards for themselves and keep them, they'll only help you in your walk with God.

We learn from those we spend time with. Are you interested in photography? Hang out with someone who is good with a camera. Do you want to be successful in business? Find someone who already is. You will learn from the people you spend the most time with. Make sure those you're investing your time in are passing on things that you want to adopt.

God, help me choose my friends and my influences wisely.
I want to better myself, not be brought down.

TENDER LOVE

"I am a God who is near," says the LORD.
"I am also a God who is far away.
No one can hide where I cannot see him," says the LORD.
"I fill all of heaven and earth," says the LORD.

JEREMIAH 23:23-24 NCV

God is so loving and tender toward us that sometimes we forget just how majestic and powerful he is. Yes, he's the God who keeps our tears in a bottle. Yes, he's the God who bends low to listen to us cry. But he's also the God who separated night from day. He's the God who sent a flood that destroyed the entire earth. He's the God who is more powerful than any devil.

As we are comforted by God's tenderness, let's not forget his greatness. His power is what makes his tenderness all the more sweet. Is there anything more precious than seeing a big strong man cradling a new baby? Something about all that power holding all that fragility is a picture of tender love—of God's love.

You are the all-powerful God. You could snuff out my life in a second. Instead, you choose to love me. You choose to hold me. You choose to be patient with me. Thank you.

RUN AWAY

*Run away from sexual sin. Every other sin people
do is outside their bodies, but those who sin
sexually sin against their own bodies.*

1 CORINTHIANS 6:18 NCV

When we're young, it can be hard to realize how our sexual behavior will affect us later in life. Sadly, this is a lesson that's often learned the hard way. If you were to ask a lot of older Christian women about some of their biggest regrets in life, this is the topic that often comes up.

When sexual immorality comes into play, there really is only one thing to do. Flee. Run away. Get out of any relationship or any situation that causes you to fall. If you continue to sin sexually, you will regret it later in life. That's a guarantee. If you've already jumped this fence and you've sinned, then ask God to build an even bigger fence around your purity. He can restore what's been lost. Use his grace to move forward in purity from this point on.

Lord, help me to stay pure. Keep me out of situations that tempt me to do something I'll spend my life regretting.

EVERLASTING LOVE

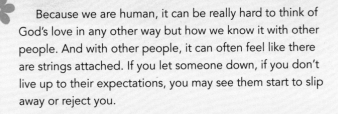

"I have loved you with an everlasting love;
I have drawn you with unfailing kindness."

JEREMIAH 31:3 NIV

Because we are human, it can be really hard to think of God's love in any other way but how we know it with other people. And with other people, it can often feel like there are strings attached. If you let someone down, if you don't live up to their expectations, you may see them start to slip away or reject you.

Though we may find this hard to believe, rejection is never the case with the Lord's love. It is unconditional. There is nothing you can do to make him turn away from you. He designed you before you were ever a wisp of your mother's imagination, and there are no strings attached to his love.

Father God, thank you for loving me unconditionally. Help me to believe that there are no strings attached to your everlasting love. I am so grateful for my relationship with you.

LISTEN TO ADVICE

Listen to advice and accept correction,
and in the end you will be wise.
PROVERBS 19:20 NCV

Advice isn't always easy to hear. We often think it means that someone is assuming they know better. Or it means they think we're wrong. Neither of those is easy to stomach. But if we don't stop and listen to correction, how can we improve? If we continue thinking that we've always got it right—which no one always does—then we'll get steadily worse.

If you're going to fail, fail forward. Learn from the mistakes you've made and become better for having made them. When someone gives advice or corrects you, it's only speeding up that process. Instead of getting annoyed, get excited when someone wants to advise or correct you. They are helping you to learn more quickly which will help you become wiser sooner.

God, help me to have a positive reaction to those who
want to correct me. Instead of being defensive, help me to
humble myself and see it as a chance to grow.

FORGIVEN AND FREE

You forgave the guilt of your people—
yes, you covered all their sins.
PSALM 85:2 NLT

We all have things in our lives we wish we could erase. Mistakes we've made, regrets we wish we didn't have to carry around. We wince when we think about them. We worry that someone will find out about what we've done and they won't forgive us. We think that God won't forgive us.

When we come to Christ, he covers all of our sin. He cloaks it in his purity. He washes it clean. He makes us come alive again as forgiven and free children of light. Our sin is covered. It's not exposed; it's not visible to all. It's hidden in his blood. That means you can walk free. Hold your head high.

God, I don't deserve to have my slate wiped clean and my sin covered. But you do it anyway because you love me and you're great. Help me to walk forward with the confidence of a forgiven and free child.

REMAIN CONNECTED

*You must remain faithful to what you have been
taught from the beginning. If you do, you will remain
in fellowship with the Son and with the Father.*

1 JOHN 2:24 NLT

Remember how it felt when you first came to know God?
Every word in the Bible jumped out at you. Every story
about God made your heart feel something—connected to
his love. Fight to keep that connection. The world will try
to rob you of it. Sin will try to come between you and God,
and the devil will try to make you think that your relationship
with him is ruined. Busyness will try to keep you from
spending time in his presence, threatening to disconnect
you from his love.

People will tell you that being a Christian isn't the best
choice. They'll tell you that God's love isn't tolerant. That
his Son died for nothing. But fight to stay faithful. Keep the
truth always in your heart. Press in to the presence of God
and sing his praises until the words of his greatness are
louder than the words of your doubt.

*God, I always want to stay connected to your love. I don't
want to lose my relationship with you because I allowed
myself to disconnect. I need you as much now as I did when
I first came to you for salvation.*

TRUE FRIENDSHIP

Accept one another, then, just as Christ accepted
you, in order to bring praise to God.

ROMANS 15:7 NIV

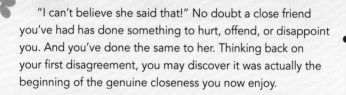

"I can't believe she said that!" No doubt a close friend you've had has done something to hurt, offend, or disappoint you. And you've done the same to her. Thinking back on your first disagreement, you may discover it was actually the beginning of the genuine closeness you now enjoy.

It's after we've seen their worst and shown our worst—and then accepted each other as is—that true friendship begins. It's the way Jesus loves us. He's been there for every poor decision, unkind thought, and selfish choice we've made, and still he chooses us. Not after we fix ourselves, but right now, just as we are. Allow his unconditional acceptance of you to inspire more love and acceptance of the people in your life.

Jesus, you know everything about me and still you love me.
Help me to accept others as you do, without condition, so
my friendships will be deep, honest, and honoring to you.

TAKING UP SPACE

Cast all your anxiety on him, because he cares for you.

1 PETER 5:7 NRSV

You're wide awake, staring at the ceiling. You check the time…again. Adding to the worry of whatever's keeping you awake, you're now anxious about the fact you're not sleeping. *What if I sleep through my alarm? What if I never fall asleep at all?*

Whether an upcoming test, a text that never came, a sick relative, or general uneasiness, anxiety is a real problem. The author of the Bible knew this, which is why so there are so many Scriptures about it. Anxiety, worry, fear, stress… whatever you call it, the solution is the same—get rid of it! Picture the thing you dread in your hand. Now toss it to Jesus. He actually *wants* your problems. Your worries are taking up space in your heart, space he wants to fill with his joy.

Lord, I hold in my hands all that keeps me from being filled with your joy. Your Word tells me to cast it on you, so here it is. Thank you, Jesus, for caring enough to take it away.

REAL BEAUTY

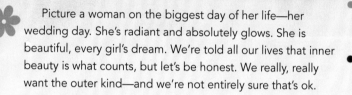

Those who look to him are radiant;
their faces are never covered with shame.

PSALM 34:5 NIV

Picture a woman on the biggest day of her life—her wedding day. She's radiant and absolutely glows. She is beautiful, every girl's dream. We're told all our lives that inner beauty is what counts, but let's be honest. We really, really want the outer kind—and we're not entirely sure that's ok.

Think about beautiful things—sunsets, flowers, fall leaves. How do they make you feel? Happy, joyful, peaceful? The most beautiful people are those you just want to be around because they make you good.

While there's nothing wrong with wanting physical beauty, beauty that radiates from within is what makes people want to be with you. That kind of beauty is entirely attainable. The more you turn to God, the more you reflect him. The joy, kindness, humility, and peace that come from knowing Jesus radiates from within you—you glow. You are beautiful.

Lord God, I want to be beautiful. I want my eyes to reflect your light and my laugh to reflect your joy. I want my smile to draw others to me, so that I can point them to you.

IT LOOKS LIKE FUN

"So he returned home to his father. And while he was still a long way off, his father saw him coming. Filled with love and compassion, he ran to his son, embraced him, and kissed him."

LUKE 15:20 NLT

Once upon a time there was a son who took the inheritance that was coming to him. Against his dad's wishes, he left his home and took off to spend his money. He had a great time—for a while. After partying and wasting all his money, though, he was soon broke and hungry. Things were so bad he started eating food meant for the pigs he took care of.

That's how sin works. It looks fun on the outside. In fact, that's what makes it a temptation. But soon it bankrupts you of all God ever created you to be. If you're in a situation where you're in a mess, realize that God is eager to forgive. Don't hesitate, wondering how God will receive you. He is waiting to welcome you back. Quickly confess your sin to the Father. Run into the power of his forgiving arms.

Father, thank you that when I confess my sin, you forgive me and embrace me, welcoming me home.

TRUTHFUL AND KIND

The wicked flee when no one pursues,
but the righteous are as bold as a lion.
PROVERBS 28:1 NRSV

If someone were to pick up your phone and start reading your messages out loud in class, what would happen? Would you be at risk of hurting friends, getting in serious trouble, being completely humiliated, or just being a little embarrassed?

No one enjoys having their privacy invaded, although having conversations revealed present more of a problem for some than for others. Whether you can hold your head high or need to duck behind a notebook depends on how closely your private self reflects your public image. Are you as honest, kind, and sincere as people perceive you to be?

If the thought of someone going through your phone has your stomach in knots, perhaps it's time to ask yourself a few questions. Are your words both truthful and kind? Do your conversations build people up, or tear them down?

Jesus, I want to be the kind of girl who could walk boldly into any room, even after all her secrets were revealed. Help me grow in kindness, truth, and love. Help me be more like you.

LEAN IN

With your help I can attack an army.
With God's help I can jump over a wall.
PSALM 18:29 NCV

Scriptures like the one above remind us of the limitless capability of God. Things that are truly impossible on our own (can *you* face an army or leap a wall?) are possible with God's help. This is incredible news, very encouraging, and often misunderstood.

All things are not guaranteed or even probable; they are *possible*. What cannot happen without the Lord *could* happen with his help. But the God of the universe doesn't always intervene. Imagine the chaos if he did! Forty girls, no matter how hard they pray, can't all get the lead in the musical. That test you didn't study for? That's on you. God makes possible the assignments *he* gives you; he helps with the dreams *he* plants in your heart. The closer you walk with him, the more you'll see him work in your life, so lean in.

Lord, I'm leaning in. Align my heart with yours, so all my dreams are from you. Show me which battles to face, which walls to jump. I want to walk with you and watch you work.

IMMEASURABLE GLORY

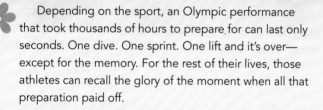

This slight momentary affliction is preparing us for
an eternal weight of glory beyond all measure.

2 CORINTHIANS 4:17 NRSV

Depending on the sport, an Olympic performance that took thousands of hours to prepare for can last only seconds. One dive. One sprint. One lift and it's over—except for the memory. For the rest of their lives, those athletes can recall the glory of the moment when all that preparation paid off.

This beautiful Scripture tells us something similar about eternity with Jesus. The troubles and hardships we face now, hard as they may be, are like training sessions. We need to be strong enough to keep in our mind the immeasurable glory and joy waiting for us in Christ. On the days life is hard, be encouraged. God has a wonderful plan for your life. The rough spots are just the workouts. Your moment of glory is coming, and it will last forever.

Jesus, life is hard sometimes! Help me remember that my sad days, my struggles, and my frustrations are there to strengthen me and prepare me for the life you have planned for me—and for eternity, where there will be more joy than I can measure.

YOU ARE CREATIVE

In his grace, God has given us different
gifts for doing certain things well.
ROMANS 12:6 NLT

Do you consider yourself talented? How about creative? Sadly, many of us believe that unless we have a gift like singing or drawing, the answer is no, but this simply isn't true! We are made in God's image, and God is incredibly creative.

Think about what you do well. What do others admire about you? Your talent may be planning memorable experiences, or making others laugh, or keeping a toddler amused. Your creativity is the way you touch and change the world around you, and it is one of the Father's favorite things about you.

Lord, I don't always see myself as creative—especially when I consider your creation. Thank you for the unique talents you gave me and for the happiness I feel when I use them. Help me discover more ways I am one of a kind, and to share and celebrate them with the world around me.

EVERY HAPPY MOMENT

*God wants all people to eat and drink and be
happy in their work, which are gifts from God.*
ECCLESIASTES 3:13 NCV

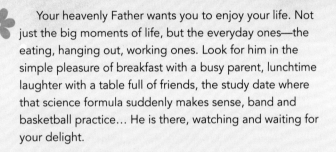

Your heavenly Father wants you to enjoy your life. Not just the big moments of life, but the everyday ones—the eating, hanging out, working ones. Look for him in the simple pleasure of breakfast with a busy parent, lunchtime laughter with a table full of friends, the study date where that science formula suddenly makes sense, band and basketball practice… He is there, watching and waiting for your delight.

Every happy moment is a gift. It's easy to forget this, especially when frustrations demand so much of our attention. Take a little time today to slow down and notice the everyday blessings God gives you.

Father God, thank you for my sweet little life. I confess to rushing right past the gifts of time with people I love, good food, and the hobbies and pastimes that make me, me. Help me to sense your presence in the laughter of friends, a snuggle with a pet, and the million other ways you choose to delight me.

LOST IN JOY

David danced before the Lord with all his might. And David was wearing a linen ephod. So David and all the house of Israel brought up the ark of the Lord with shouting and with the sound of the horn.

2 SAMUEL 6:14-15 ESV

The David in the verse above is King David, ruler of Israel. He's just fulfilled a long-term goal, and he's overjoyed, dancing before the Lord with all his might. Stop for a moment and imagine what this scene might look like today. Picture the president completely lost in a celebratory dance, praising God. It's difficult to imagine, isn't it? You may even be laughing a little bit at the thought of it.

David had his share of shocked bystanders too. Even his own wife was embarrassed by his display. But here's the beauty of the story: the king didn't care. David was lost in joy. The only opinion that mattered to him was God's opinion, and God wanted him to dance.

God, how wonderful it would be to know you as David did! Help me to worship you freely, and lose myself in your joy.

BIGGER, BETTER, MORE

You are rich in everything—in faith, in speaking,
in knowledge, in truly wanting to help, and in
the love you learned from us. In the same way,
be strong also in the grace of giving.

2 CORINTHIANS 8:7 NCV

When we think of having everything, what comes to mind? Beautiful clothes, big house, fancy car, and endless gadgets. What else? Good looks and talent? In this letter to the Corinthians, the apostle Paul mentions none of these. Were the standards of "richness" so different back then, or was it Paul who was different?

Paul talks about being rich in faith, knowledge, and even in giving. How close are we to having—or even wanting—this biblical description of wealth? What would our lives look like if we dreamed of having bigger faith instead of bigger houses, a beautiful testimony instead of a beautiful wardrobe? If our hearts burned for more time to serve instead of more electronics, how rich could we be?

Father, I confess I like the shiny things the world has to offer, and I often find myself wanting more—wishing I were richer. I want to be rich by heaven's standards. Help me see "having everything" the way you see it, God.

GOD IS FOREVER

We do not look at the things which are seen, but at the things which are not seen. For the things which are seen are temporary, but the things which are not seen are eternal.

2 CORINTHIANS 4:18 NKJV

Have you ever been so angry with a friend you thought you might never forgive her, only to realize a few days later you're enjoying each other again? Or felt as though your heart was broken beyond repair, only to laugh about it a few weeks later, wondering how you could have possibly been that sad over something (or someone) so silly?

One of the things your heavenly Father wants you to understand is that from his perspective, everything here on earth will eventually seem like that broken heart—temporary. God is forever. That's how long he has loved you and how long he will keep on loving you.

Father God, on the days the things I can see are too much for me to bear, help me remember all the beautiful, unseen things you have planned for me. Remind me that I am your beloved daughter, today and forever.

WAIT

Be joyful in hope, patient in affliction, faithful in prayer.
ROMANS 12:12 NIV

Do you enjoy waiting? Most of us don't enjoy it, but what if we could? We spend much of our lives hoping, waiting, and praying for things that haven't yet happened. How great would it be if that time were joyful, filled with patience and faith?

This short verse in Romans is overflowing with encouragement for times of waiting. While you hope, be joyful. In other words, expect the thing you hope for. Anticipate it. If you're suffering, be patient. Relax, rest, and know your time of affliction will end. While you pray, be filled with faith. Believe in God's willingness to grant your heart's desires, and continue to bring them before him. Try it, and see if your perspective on waiting changes.

Lord, waiting is so hard! Whether I'm in a hurry or afraid what I wait for may not happen, I find myself anxious and impatient. Thank you for this verse and its reminder to slow down and anticipate the time you'll fulfill my longing and answer my prayers. Fill me with faith as I wait and hope.

TAKE IT AWAY

The LORD is my light and my salvation—
so why should I be afraid?
PSALM 27:1 NLT

"Don't be mad, but..." When someone starts a conversation with this, we know what that person means is, "I really don't want you to be mad at me, but I did something you won't like." Conversely, "Don't laugh" means "I know this is funny, but I really don't want you to laugh at me." When someone asks us not to feel something, they are telling us something about how *they* feel. They are letting us in.

The Bible gives many such insights, especially when it comes to fear. When you feel fear creeping into your heart, imagine God whispering in your ear, "I know this is scary, my sweet daughter, but I hate seeing you like this. I'm strong enough for both of us; let me take your fear away."

Dear Lord, when I become fearful, draw me close and
remind me of how deeply you love me. Help me focus on
you and your strength while my fear fades away.

KNOWN FOR WHAT

"Don't judge others, and you will not be judged. Don't accuse others of being guilty, and you will not be accused of being guilty. Forgive, and you will be forgiven."

LUKE 6:37 NCV

Have you ever been wrong? Of course you have. We all have. You make a decision and within moments you know you shouldn't have done it. You say something, and the second it leaves your mouth you know you shouldn't have said it.

While you may have made poor choices, you didn't become a bad person. You became a person in need of compassion, forgiveness, and grace. When someone says or does something wrong, quickly trade places with them in your heart so you can give them the same understanding you'd want them to give you. Be the kind of person who is known for compassion, forgiveness, and grace so that when you need it (and you will!), it will be given to you.

Perfect Lord, I confess to judging people based on their choices, though I'd never want someone to judge me that way. Help me to see others as you see them. I want to be known as you are, for grace, forgiveness, and endless compassion.

FREE TO GO

*The Lord is the Spirit, and where the Spirit
of the Lord is, there is freedom.*

2 CORINTHIANS 3:17 NRSV

If you've had many opportunities to share your faith, you've undoubtedly had someone wonder if they would have to give up their freedom—or stop having fun—in order to follow Jesus. Maybe you've even had such thoughts yourself. What does it mean to be free in Christ?

Once we choose to walk with Jesus, he gives us his Holy Spirit. Think of him as a best friend—with perfect judgment and great taste. When the Lord is the most important thing in your life, the Holy Spirit guides you, pointing you toward things that are good for you. Anywhere he points, you are free to go. Note: This isn't an excuse to go wild and do whatever *you* want. It's a freedom to move with the Spirit toward what *God* wants. So…the closer we stay to Jesus, the more freedom we have.

God, I crave your Spirit. I want to walk so closely to Jesus that I want only what you want for me. I pray your voice and influence would drown out all others, so I can be truly free.

SHARPENED

As iron sharpens iron,
so a friend sharpens a friend.
PROVERBS 27:17 NLT

Think a moment about your best friends. What is it about them that makes them so special to you? Have you ever noticed that you like yourself best when you're with your closest friends?

One of the sweetest gifts of friendship is becoming our best selves. Our friends' humor, compassion, sense of adventure, generosity, and enthusiasm leave an imprint on us. And we affect them as well. Just by being there for one another, we make each other better.

Lord God, thank you for my friends. Friends present and past have all left a mark on me. The wonderful ways you made them have made me a better me, and the unique and intentional ways you shaped me have influenced them as well. I'm so grateful for the care you take in choosing who to place in my life.

JUST BECAUSE

From his fullness we have all received, grace upon grace.
JOHN 1:16 ESV

Don't you love "just because" gifts? No holiday, no achievement, no birthday, just a gift—just because. Whether it was store bought gift, a heartfelt letter, or unasked-for favor, it has the same, wonderful effect. A gift you weren't expecting or don't deserve makes you feel particularly special.

These unmerited, "just-because" offerings are a perfect illustration of God's grace. We all are welcome to the undeserved forgiveness offered through Jesus' sacrifice on the cross. On top of that, each and every day God shows us grace for our mistakes, blesses us, and involves himself in our concerns. We don't earn it; in fact, we don't deserve it at all. Just because he loves us, just because he delights in us, just because he feels like it, the Lord heaps grace on top of grace. Who can you surprise with grace today?

Jesus I will never get over what you did for us—for me— when you sacrificed your life for all my sins. I don't deserve your grace, but just because you love me, you give it again and again. Thank you.

WHERE YOU SEND ME

The LORD says, "I will make you wise
and show you where to go.
I will guide you and watch over you."
PSALM 32:8 NCV

"What should I do?" The older we get, the more often we find ourselves asking this question. We ask our friends, parents, teachers, coaches, and even the air. But how often do we ask God? More importantly, do we ask expecting an answer, prepared to listen?

God wants to be the first person on your list. The more important the decision, the more vital it is to go to him in focused, sincere prayer. Ask him to lead you toward the best advisors and to reveal the right choices. Be ready and willing to follow his lead when you feel his nudge or sense his wisdom.

Father, what should I do? Because you love me, I trust your guidance. Help me hear your voice. Guide me as I seek advice from people who know you and who want what's best for me, not just people who will tell me what I want to hear. Make me wise, God, and show me where to go.

CALLED PRECIOUS

*Once again you will have compassion on us.
You will trample our sins under your feet
and throw them into the depths of the ocean!*

MICAH 7:19 NLT

I can't believe I did it again! What is it about certain sins and behaviors that keep us coming back? Why don't we learn? Why don't we stop? You'd think a healthy dose of guilt would do the trick, but it doesn't. Be careful now. Behind guilt often follows an unhealthy helping of shame. *I'm a terrible person.*

Darling girl, if this is you, pay attention. Guilt, or recognizing your sins, is healthy. It's a chance to confess to God and receive forgiveness. Shame, or letting your sins define you, is toxic. Your Father smashes your sins under his feet; he tosses them to the bottom of the ocean! He sends them away precisely because they *don't* define you. *He* defines you. And he calls you precious.

Father, help me remember that I am not my sins! I confess them to you. Thank you for taking them away. Your love and compassion define me, and they are priceless.

MORE LIKE YOU

*Whoever has this world's goods, and sees his
brother in need, and shuts up his heart from him,
how does the love of God abide in him?*

1 JOHN 3:17 NKJV

When we're little, our understanding of the Bible is fairly
contained. God made the world. Noah built a huge boat
and took the animals on a trip. Jesus loves me. If I pray and
ask him into my heart, I will go to heaven. Then we grow
up, and encounter verses like the one above. They make us
uncomfortable.

The truth is, God sometimes wants us to be
uncomfortable. In this case, uncomfortable enough to be
bothered because someone else is in need. He wants us
to care more about others than ourselves. Because we are
human, this is difficult. So what do we do? Recognize how
far we have to go—how far we will always have to go—and
ask him, "What can I do today to grow more like you?"

*Lord, I have so much, yet sharing is hard. I even find myself
wanting more. I realize how generous and perfect your heart
is, and how desperately I need your love to live in me. Teach
me how to love like you.*

A SINGLE SPOT

"Whoever can be trusted with very little can also be trusted with much, and whoever is dishonest with very little will also be dishonest with much."

LUKE 16:10 NIV

If you've ever owned an item of white clothing, you know a single spot of grape juice, spaghetti sauce, or Sharpie ink can ruin the whole garment. Lies and betrayal are like those stains: a single incident can discolor an entire friendship.

If your friend can't be trusted to keep a harmless secret, like what you got another friend for a gift, how can you trust her with an important secret? If your friend is willing to lie about her plans in order to spend time with one friend over another, why should you believe her about anything else?

Honest people are honest. Trustworthy people are trustworthy. Consider this as you make your decisions about who to spend your time with and every time you are tempted to tell a half-truth or disclose a secret.

God, thank you for the wonderful advice in your Word! As I learn about who you are, I also learn about who I want to be—and who I want to be around.

HE WANTS IT ALL

*Devote yourselves to prayer with an
alert mind and a thankful heart.*

COLOSSIANS 4:2 NLT

It's happened to all of us. "Yep. Sounds good," we say. Then an uncomfortable silence. We look up from our phones, the TV, or whatever it was that had the majority of our attention and face the person we thought we were agreeing with. "You have no idea what I said, do you?" they ask. Embarrassed and apologetic, we admit it. We were going through the motions.

How often do our conversations with Jesus look like this? We're singing in church only to realize our thoughts have gone completely off on their own. We close our eyes and clasp our hands to pray, but our hearts are elsewhere. Jesus doesn't want half of our attention; he wants it all. When we pray, let's pray giving ourselves completely to connecting with his Spirit. When we thank him for our blessings, let's consider the giver of all blessings.

Father, forgive me for praying with half a mind and expressing thanks with half a heart. You are the giver of every good gift, and you deserve all my attention, gratitude, and praise.

SEPTEMBER

Be on guard.

Stand firm in the faith.

Be courageous.

Be strong.

And do everything with love.

1 CORINTHIANS 16:13–14 NLT

JUST BE THERE

*They sat down with him on the ground seven days
and seven nights, and no one spoke a word to
him, for they saw that his grief was very great.*

JOB 2:13 NKJV

When someone is going through a tragedy, we don't always know what to do. We're used to passing out opinions and encouragement, so we may think we have to say something in order to be helpful. It can be tempting to repeat old clichés, like, "Everything happens for a reason," and, "God doesn't give us more than we can handle."

Here's another option. Tell the truth. Tell them you're sorry, and you have no idea what to say. Rather than trying to fix the situation, just be there. If you read the book of Job, you'll see that his friends got a lot of things wrong, but this one they got right. When they saw at first how great his sorrow was, no one said a word.

Father God, your Word is amazing. Everything I need to know about love is contained in its pages. Today I learned that sometimes the best thing to say is nothing. Thank you for this wisdom, and may I remember it when the time comes.

FOREVER MADE PERFECT

By that one offering he forever made perfect
those who are being made holy.
HEBREWS 10:14 NLT

When was the last time you looked at something and said, "It's perfect!" How about yourself? Assuming you are like the overwhelming majority of teenage girls—or women of any age—you spend a great deal more time considering your flaws than admiring your perfection. It may even feel wrong to think of yourself as perfect, but guess what? That's exactly how God thinks of you.

There will be time enough tomorrow to go back to thinking of all the ways you can improve, so just for today, maybe even just for now, breathe in this beautiful truth: "I am perfect. I don't have to add one thing to who I am in order to be accepted by the Maker of heaven and earth. He is satisfied with me and I am made perfect."

Father God, I can't really wrap my mind around this one, but I am going to try. You made me exactly as I am. Even when sin stained me, you made a way through Jesus to make me perfect. How can I thank you for that other than to agree?

PLEASING PEOPLE

Do you think I am trying to make people accept me? No, God is the One I am trying to please. Am I trying to please people? If I still wanted to please people, I would not be a servant of Christ.

GALATIANS 1:10 NCV

How important is fitting in? (You can be honest—God already knows.) If you're not sure, here's something to think about: how many different yous are there? Think about home-with-the-family you. How different is she from the sports-team you, the lunchroom you, or the alone you? It's normal to want approval, but the more yous there are, the more likely it is that you're too wrapped up in what others think.

The apostle Paul realized early in his ministry that there would always be someone who didn't like what he was saying or doing, so he chose to seek the approval of God alone. The result? He was happy—all the time. Even in prison, Paul experienced the joy of knowing he was pleasing the only one he cared to impress.

Father God, help me remember that being my true self and living to please you is the best way to a happy life!

ENTIRELY LOVELY

*The LORD said to Samuel, "Do not consider his appearance
or his height, for I have rejected him. The LORD does not
look at the things people look at. People look at the
outward appearance, but the LORD looks at the heart."*

1 SAMUEL 16:7 NIV

A 2001 movie featured a character hypnotized so he
would see people as attractive or unattractive depending
on what kind of people they were, rather than on what
physical beauty they had. As a result, he fell deeply in love
with a woman he never would have looked at twice. The film
was heart-warming, thought-provoking…and completely
unrealistic.

Spend five minutes in nature, and you'll see that God is
as in love with beautiful things as anyone. After all, he gave
us our sense of beauty. He wants his creation to be enjoyed.
However, when it comes to people, appearance is not his
first priority—and he doesn't want it to be ours. More than
anything, the Lord cares about our hearts.

*Father, examine my heart and show me how to be more
beautiful in your eyes. I want to be lovely to you.*

WHO WE FOLLOW

Let your eyes look straight ahead;
fix your gaze directly before you.
PROVERBS 4:25 NIV

When a promising young student or athlete doesn't reach their potential, we say they must have "taken their eyes off the ball" or "lost sight of the prize." When someone makes a mistake, people say things like they "got off track" or they "lost their way."

All these expressions imply that our lives are on a path, and the best way to succeed is to stay focused. We all start out wanting to be good, to live with integrity. Turning our gaze toward worldly concerns in media and popular culture are a great way to stumble off that path. Recognizing this, then fixing our eyes firmly on Christ, is a wonderful way to remember where we are going, and with whom.

Lord, everywhere I look there are things that tempt me to take my eyes off you and the life I want to lead. The world tells me it's all about me, but I know that isn't true. Help me fix my gaze on you. Lead me down the path of integrity.

WHAT BREAKS HIS HEART

Let justice roll down like waters
And righteousness like an ever-flowing stream.

AMOS 5:24 NASB

Somewhere very near you, this very night, is a girl with no home. She is your age. She might even share your name or your birthday. People older and more powerful than her have taken her freedom, her innocence, and her security.

It's heartbreaking. It's wrong. It's so very, very unfair. But what can you do? To begin with, you can *care*. God wants our hearts to break for what breaks his, and this girl's story is *crushing him*. Take these words from Amos and pray them for her, for all the girls in this cruel, broken world who find themselves in a desperate, ugly situation. Raise your voice to God, who loves her just as much as he loves you, and pray that through others who also care, her hope will be restored.

Lord, there are so many injustices in this world that I sometimes just want to cover my head and pretend they aren't true. But as someone who loves Jesus, I know you want more from me. Bring justice to the exploited, God. Free their bodies and heal their hearts.

WHO YOU LOVE

*Dear children, let us not love with words or
speech but with actions and in truth.*

1 JOHN 3:18 NIV

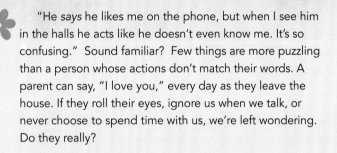

"He *says* he likes me on the phone, but when I see him
in the halls he acts like he doesn't even know me. It's so
confusing." Sound familiar? Few things are more puzzling
than a person whose actions don't match their words. A
parent can say, "I love you," every day as they leave the
house. If they roll their eyes, ignore us when we talk, or
never choose to spend time with us, we're left wondering.
Do they really?

Jesus taught that love is about what we do, and he
modeled this with his ministry. He didn't tell the sick people,
"Oh, I feel so bad for you! Get well soon!" He healed them.
He didn't say, "Oh, no food? Bummer!" He fed them. Who
do *you* love, and how do they know?

*Lord, I don't want anyone to wonder if my love is for real.
Inspire me to help, to encourage, and to pour myself into
my relationships. Help me love not just with my words but
with my whole life.*

HE WANTS YOU

I want you to show love, not offer sacrifices.
I want you to know me more than I want burnt offerings.

HOSEA 6:6 NLT

How close would you feel to someone who never made time to hang out or even talk to you but who kept sending you expensive presents? Honestly, it would get a little weird, right? Friendship comes from experience not from gift bags.

God is no different. If we're not spending time in prayer and actively seeking Jesus' presence in our daily lives, we can't expect to feel the Holy Spirit because we sing along during worship and put half our babysitting money in the offering basket. God doesn't want your $20 bills and for your voice to be the loudest—he wants you.

Jesus, forgive me for trying to impress you with my generosity and my spirituality when I know what you really want is my heart. I want to know you, Lord, and I want you to know me. Help me seek you and sense you all the time. Help me appreciate what a gift your presence is—so much more than any present I can bring.

BEST FRIENDS

A man of too many friends comes to ruin,
But there is a friend who sticks closer than a brother.
PROVERBS 18:24 NASB

How many friends do you have? It depends, right? Are we talking social media friends, big party friends, sleepover friends, or 24/7 besties? The importance of the question is less about the numbers than a clear understanding of friendship. If we mistakenly classify too many people as "best friends," the term becomes meaningless—and so, perhaps, do the relationships.

Who would you get up for in the middle of the night? Who would get up for you? Who knows everything about you, even the ugly bits, and adores you anyway? Being a true friend—closer than a brother or a sister—requires an investment of time, trust, and heart. If we try to pour ourselves into too many people, no one gets our best.

Lord, you wired us for love, and I love my friends. No matter how I count or classify them, help me understand friendship and appreciate the gift of those rare, beautiful ones you chose to be my 24/7s. Their unconditional acceptance gives me a taste of your love, and it's so very sweet.

LOVELY GARDEN

The entire law is fulfilled in keeping this one
command: "Love your neighbor as yourself."
If you bite and devour each other, watch out
or you will be destroyed by each other.

GALATIANS 5:15 NIV

Girls fight, right? Even if you manage to stay mostly out of it, someone close to you is probably living this right now. Rather than trying to figure out who is right, let's be encouraged by this verse to choose peace. It's a powerful image. Picturing our arguments as bites out of one another, we can easily see the danger—eventually, there will be nothing left.

Considered less graphically, imagine a garden. Your fights are flowers torn from the ground, and your forgiveness and grace are new plantings. At the end of the season which area of the garden will be lovelier? Where will you more easily sense God's presence?

Lord, you love peace because you love us. You want what's best for us, and you know that fighting and disagreements tear us apart and kill our roots. Forgiveness and grace allow us to flourish and grow and be more aware of your presence and love. Help me remember this, God, so I can continue to grow closer to you.

WHY I AM HERE

*Some cried out one thing, some another, for the
assembly was in confusion, and most of them
did not know why they had come together.*
ACTS 19:32 ESV

There are days when this verse could be describing the
entire teenage experience. It's so easy to get swept up in
the emotion of our peers, raising our voices simply to be
heard, only to realize we're not even sure what we're so
worked up about. *Wait. How did the situation between
these two people become my problem? What am I even
doing here?* we wonder.

It's an excellent question, and one best asked of the
Father. Is your participation adding something of benefit?
Is your behavior representing Jesus' love? Are your words
honoring? If not, go home.

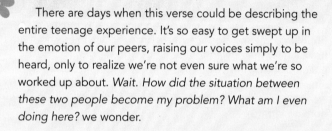

*Lord Jesus, half the time I actually don't know why I get
involved. I allow other people's business to become mine
then try to take your place and tell them how to live. I shout
more to be heard than to bring you glory. Remind me who I
am, Jesus, and who you are! Let me draw others and bring
honor to you. When I don't, send me home.*

BECAUSE HE IS GOD

Give unto the LORD the glory due to His name;
Worship the LORD in the beauty of holiness.

PSALM 29:2 NKJV

There are at least a million reasons to worship God, and each day he adds to them by forgiving us, blessing us, and dazzling us with his power, glory, and beauty. No matter how much we write down, recall, or read about, we can never come close to identifying all the reasons he is worthy of our praise.

So let's give it him. Because he's God and because he's holy, give him the glory he deserves. Spend some time customizing your prayer today: share what's in your heart.

God I thank you for_____. I'm astonished by the beauty of_____, and I can never repay the grace you show me. Forgive me for_____, and help me to wake each new day filled with amazement, gratitude, and praise. You are God, and you are worthy.

TO BE KNOWN

Is anyone among you suffering? Let him pray.
Is anyone cheerful? Let him sing psalms.
JAMES 5:13 NKJV

How is your prayer life? Perhaps you recite memorized prayers. Or maybe you find yourself blurting out your needs and asking for help as they arise or thanking him for blessings large and small when you recognize them. Maybe you have a journal filled with letters to the Father. All of these are equally pleasing to God, provided you are coming to him with an open heart and focused mind.

Prayer is simply talking with God. As many ways as there are to converse, there are ways to pray. He wants to know how you feel about him, what you're sorry for, what you're grateful for, and what you need. He wants to know what you fear, what you dream, and what you wonder about. Like a good and loving father, he wants to know his daughter.

Father God, when I think of all the people in the world, I'm amazed that you are so interested in me. You long for my love, you forgive my sins, you shower me with blessings and you help me with my needs. How can this be, and how can I thank you?

THE WORLD IS WRONG

*Pray for us, for our conscience is clear and we
want to live honorably in everything we do.*

HEBREWS 13:18 NLT

The world is not interested in your purity. Society doesn't
want your wedding night to be the sacred, special miracle
God intended. Try to name three admired and respected
celebrities who have chosen to keep themselves pure for
their future spouses. It's not easy, is it? Our culture would
have you believe sex is all about pleasure and the natural,
expected expression between two people who find each
other attractive.

But the world is wrong. More desperately than you can
imagine, God wants you to experience intimacy the way he
designed it. Talk to your friends about purity, and commit to
pray for one another regularly. Your desire to live honorably
is precious and beautiful to God, and he wants you to
succeed. Your purity is a gift you can only give once. Don't
let anyone tell you differently.

*God, the older I get, the more I will need your protection
and your strength to keep me pure. Help me wait no matter
what the world says.*

NOT LOST

If I go up to the heavens, you are there;
if I make my bed in the depths, you are there.
If I rise on the wings of the dawn,
if I settle on the far side of the sea,
even there your hand will guide me,
your right hand will hold me fast.

PSALM 139:8-10 NIV

Depending on our mood or intentions, this passage can be a little frustrating. The truth: we can't get away from God. Ever. That thing we don't want him to see? He sees. Always. If we follow through and do it anyway? Then we just need to turn to him for forgiveness.

Alternatively, these same verses can also bring tremendous comfort. The fear that you're so lost even God can't find you? Never gonna happen. Again, the truth: we can't get away from God. There is no such thing as lost. We just need to turn to him and let him scoop us up in his arms.

Lord, you're always there. When I sin and try to hide, you see me and forgive me before I even ask. When I think I might be lost, you stand behind me with open arms. Thank you, God, for never letting me go.

PATIENCE OVER POWER

Better to be patient than powerful;
better to have self-control than to conquer a city.
PROVERBS 16:32 NLT

Read the verse again, and think about it for a few moments. Do you believe what it's saying? How might patience be better than power?

Jesus' ministry sheds a brilliant light. Think about who Jesus was. He was God—in the flesh! Being God, did he have to *walk around* for three whole years talking to and healing small groups of people? Couldn't he just tap into all that power and transport himself and the disciples wherever he wanted to go? While we're thinking about it, couldn't he just have forced everyone to obey him?

Of course he could have done all these things and more. Yet Jesus chose patience over power, self-control over conquering. Why? Because he wants friends, not slaves. God wants to know us, not to own us, and relationships take time.

Lord, I don't always want to learn to be patient. I just want to be there already. Thank you for Jesus' example. Life with you is about relationships, and relationships require patience. Thank you, too, for your patience with me.

273

GOD DOESN'T WANDER

Seek the LORD and His strength;
Seek His face evermore!
PSALM 105:4 NKJV

Wouldn't it be nice to feel the way we do after a great praise concert or youth retreat all the time? When we feel God's Spirit, the strength of the Lord is ours and we can answer any challenge, face any obstacle, or stay calm thorough any storm.

Then life happens. Tests and practices and chores happen, and God's face grows a little blurry. We feel his power start to drain from our veins. This is a good thing! Yes, you read that right. It's good because it reminds us of what we want—of who we want—and it highlights our distraction. He wants us seeking, ever searching for him. If you can't feel him, turn toward him. He's not the one who wandered; you are.

God, I forget how this works sometimes. You don't follow me; I follow you. When I can't feel you I think you've left me, but you haven't—you never do. I'm the one who wanders. You are the one who remains and invites me to turn around and seek you out.

PRIMARY DISTRACTION

Rejoice always, pray without ceasing, in everything give thanks; for this is the will of God in Christ Jesus for you.

1 THESSALONIANS 5:16-18 NKJV

This one's easy: Rejoice. Pray. Give thanks. No problem. And it would be, if that were all it said. Rejoice *always*. Pray *without ceasing*. *In everything* give thanks. Hmm. That changes things. How do you do that? Rejoice when you're sad, angry, frustrated? Pray when you're watching TV, studying, or laughing with friends? Give thanks for cancelled plans, pop quizzes, and rejection?

God knows you can't think of him every second, but he does want to be your first and last thought, your number one priority, and the primary distraction from every frustration in your life. Angry? Acknowledge it then rejoice that you don't have to stay that way. Studying? Take a break and pray for a clear head. Didn't make the team? Mourn your loss then thank him for the opportunity to spend more time with your family and friends.

God, you're amazing. Even your commands are meant to bring me more joy. When life hurts, you invite me to turn my thoughts to you. When I do, how can I stay down?

ALTOGETHER DIFFERENT

Have mercy on me, O God, because of your unfailing love.
Because of your great compassion,
blot out the stain of my sins.

PSALM 51:1 NLT

If you've grown up following God and obeying his commands, it might be hard for you to watch others turn their back on him. People that you once knew loved God seem to have walked away. You might be wondering, How does God view people like that? What does he think of them?

King David, someone who was described as a person after God's own heart, turned his back on God for a time. He stole and had someone murdered. What did God think of him? Well, God loved him enough to send someone to confront David. God is altogether different than we are. Where our patience has run out, his loving kindness and persevering love are still running at full throttle. Instead of criticizing others, we have the privilege of continuing to show God's unfailing love to those who've turned away from him. Maybe the love we show them will bring them back to God.

Father, thank you for your heart of compassion and for welcoming even the most rebellious person back to you. Help me to show that same compassion to others.

DEEPLY LOVED

"If a man has a hundred sheep but one of the sheep
gets lost, he will leave the other ninety-nine on the
hill and go to look for the lost sheep. I tell you the
truth, if he finds it he is happier about that one sheep
than about the ninety-nine that were never lost."

MATTHEW 18:12-13 NCV

Whose love do you question the least? Whoever they are
and whatever they have done for you, know that it's nothing
compared to what God would do to make sure you know
how deeply he loves you.

Your heavenly Father's love has no limits. Do you believe
this? Can you grasp it? There is nothing you can do to
change his mind about you. You don't have to become any
more lovable, intelligent, beautiful, capable, generous, or
anything else. He loves you so much that if you wander off,
he will drop everything to bring you back.

*Lord God, this knowledge is almost too much for me.
Realizing how deeply you love me shows me how much
room I have to grow in my love for you. I want to be
desperate for you, Father. Fill me with that desire.*

IT HAS TO BE HIM

*If I must boast, I will boast of the things
that show my weakness.*
2 CORINTHIANS 11:30 NIV

"I got an A on my test." "I won first place!" "I made the cheerleading team." Those are the kind of things we boast about. No one boasts about their weaknesses, only their strengths. Strengths are what *we* can do.

That's why Paul, in the verse above, says he boasts about his weaknesses. He knew that weaknesses give God the opportunity to show up and do what *he* can do. When we do well at something we know we're not good at on our own—like being patient or kind or loving—then it *has to be* God at work, right? Like when you've always been a little selfish and suddenly find yourself wanting to share. You know your natural tendency, so that sweet new impulse? It's all him.

God, today I thank you for my flaws and weaknesses because they give me a chance to see you at work. When I see myself succeeding in a new area, especially if love is involved, I know it's you—and I can't wait to share.

A SOURCE YOU CAN TRUST

Faith comes from hearing, and hearing through the word of Christ.

ROMANS 10:17 ESV

Rumors are just rumors until you hear it for yourself from a source you trust. Anyone who ever played "telephone" as a young girl knows how words can get twisted and changed as they go from one person to the next. If you want to know if your friend really said or did what she's being accused of, ask her.

The same goes for God. We can't call him up and ask him, but we can read his sacred text and find out what he said. Everything he ever said, did, or wants us to know is written down and available for our study. Our faith in God grows by hearing what he did, who he is, and what he says. Our source is the Bible. Need more faith? Read the Word. Need more truth, guidance, and wisdom? They're all there.

God, thank you for making sure that everything I need to know is written in your Word. Guide me toward the lessons and truths you most want me to learn. Help my faith to grow.

WAITING FOR PERFECTION

Those who wait for perfect weather
will never plant seeds;
those who look at every cloud
will never harvest crops.

ECCLESIASTES 11:4 NCV

If we waited for things to be perfect, would anything ever happen? If our skin had to be flawless and every hair in place, would we ever leave the house? If our skills had to be Olympian, would we ever try out for the team? Of course not. We know all this, but we also forget.

The same is true for sharing God with others. Let's not think we have to be spiritually mature before we start up the Bible study, sinless before we invite someone to church, or have the Bible memorized before we share our testimony. God calls us as we are to stand up, speak out, and share his love. Let's do it.

Lord, thank you for reminding me I don't have to be perfect in order to share you with others. No one else who loves you is perfect either, and that is such a relief. Give me the boldness to see past the clouds, scatter my seeds, and watch you make them grow.

HE KNOWS

We do not know how to pray as we should. But the Spirit himself speaks to God for us, even begs God for us with deep feelings that words cannot explain.

ROMANS 8:26 NCV

Have you ever been so hungry you couldn't decide what you wanted? Yes to one thing means no to everything else, and *it all sounds so good!* "What do I want?" you ask, of no one in particular.

Prayer can be like that too. Sometimes we have so many feelings and questions and needs, we don't even know what to say. Wonderfully, we don't have to say anything. This is one of the many benefits of the Holy Spirit. Because he lives in us, he knows us as well as we know ourselves—even better—and he can interpret all those moans and groans for God and ask just what we need. Even when we're not sure what that is.

Holy Spirit, I don't always know what I want. Even when I think I do, you know better. You know me so intimately and care for me so deeply, that all my needs can get through to you, especially when I can't even say what they are.

281

CHOOSING WELL

"Today I have given you the choice between life and death, between blessings and curses. Now I call on heaven and earth to witness the choice you make. Oh, that you would choose life, so that you and your descendants might live!"

DEUTERONOMY 30:19 NLT

God is intimately interested in your choices. He may not be on the edge of his seat wondering if you'll have a PB&J or a turkey sandwich for lunch, but make no mistake, that decision to cheat or not, lie or be truthful, date or wait, he can't wait to see what you decide.

You know God has plans for you, but do you also know that the final choice rests with you? He guides and directs but you decide, and all of heaven and earth are waiting to see how it turns out.

Lord, sometimes I wish I didn't have to choose. I wish you'd just make the hard decisions for me, but I know that's not how it works. Thank you for my freedom to choose and for guiding me to choose well.

SURRENDER TO FREEDOM

O LORD, you are our Father.
We are the clay, and you are the potter.
ISAIAH 64:8 NLT

How does the word *surrender* make you feel? For a lot of us, it isn't necessarily a positive concept. We think of defeated armies, guilty criminals, and helpless prisoners. Surrender seems a little scary. And it can be, when you're on opposing sides.

God is on our side, so to him, surrender means something entirely different. Surrender to God equals freedom. We spend much of our lives, whether we realize it or not, resisting God. We think we know what's best, and we struggle to make our plans work out.

When we surrender to God, we give up the striving. We let him take over. His plan becomes our plan. When you remember how much he loves you, you realize there's nothing scary about that.

God, help me surrender. I'm young so it may take me some time to really get this one, but I want to get it! I want your will to be my will and your plan to be my plan. Remind me you want what's best for me. Because of that, I don't ever have to struggle or resist you.

DIRECT MY STEPS

Direct my footsteps according to your word;
let no sin rule over me.
PSALM 119:133 NIV

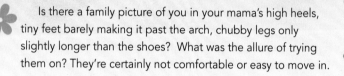

Is there a family picture of you in your mama's high heels, tiny feet barely making it past the arch, chubby legs only slightly longer than the shoes? What was the allure of trying them on? They're certainly not comfortable or easy to move in.

We all want to feel elegant and those narrow, pointy pumps seem to be the ticket. Now that you're older, you've probably stepped out in your own high heels. How was it? A little wobbly?

Stepping out in our faith is a little like walking in heels. At first, we're shaky and uncertain. Everywhere we look, ladies seem to be in taller, pointier, prettier shoes, making it look a whole lot easier than we are. (It's ok; she's teetering too.) That's another reason we have the Holy Spirit. The Helper is a strong, steady arm, directing our steps, keeping us steady in the God's Word and steering us away from sin.

Holy Spirit, I need your strong, steady arm to guide me and keep me on the right path. This walk is beautiful; I wouldn't trade it for anything. But I'd be lying if I said it was always easy or pain free. Thank you for being here to hold me up.

THROUGH THE STORM

*"Anyone who listens to my teaching and follows it
is wise, like a person who builds a house on solid
rock. Though the rain comes in torrents and the
floodwaters rise and the winds beat against that house,
it won't collapse because it is built on bedrock."*

MATTHEW 7:24-25 NLT

Everyone loves a good story. And Jesus was a master
storyteller. In this parable, two people built different houses.
One house was built on sand and the other on rock. When
rain poured down, floods rose, and the winds whipped up
around the house built on rock, the house stood firm. When
the rain poured down on the house built on sand, the house
collapsed. Neither home was exempt from the storm.

Precious one, even as a child of God—even as a *wise*
child of God—you'll experience storms. The temptation is
to blame yourself or say, "Why is this happening to me? I
must have done something wrong." Good and bad things
happen to everyone. What's different is God's presence and
peace in the storm. You don't need to be afraid. Call on the
name of Jesus, and he will give you the stability you need
when all else is shaking.

*Father, thanks for the promise of your presence even in the
storms of life. Help me build my foundation on you, my
rock, so when storms come, I don't need to be afraid.*

THE NARROW GATE

*"Heaven can be entered only through the narrow gate!
The highway to hell is broad, and its gate is wide enough
for all the multitudes who choose its easy way."*

MATTHEW 7:13-14 TLB

Who would choose to do something hard over
something easy? No one, right? Yet for the right reward,
doing something hard might be totally worth it. Practicing
gymnastics for eight hours a day might mean a gold medal.
Researching for a paper for an afternoon might mean
getting an A.

In these verses, Jesus describes two roads, one that's
wide and another that's narrow. The wide path is easy. It
means doing what you want, when you want, how you want,
even if that means going against what God says. The narrow
path can be more difficult. It means following Jesus even
when it's not popular. But the payoff? It's huge!

First comes the reward of God's presence. He's
walking right along with you on that narrow path, and he's
everything that's good and kind. Then there's the reward of
heaven, living with him throughout all eternity. Choosing the
right path, and sticking to it, is a choice you won't regret.

*Father, help me keep doing right when doing what's wrong
seems so much easier. Thank you that you reward those who
persevere.*

INCREDIBLE INHERITANCE

*It is by his great mercy that we have been born again....
Now we live with great expectation, and we have a priceless
inheritance—an inheritance that is kept in heaven for you,
pure and undefiled, beyond the reach of change and decay.*

1 PETER 1:4 NLT

Imagine the phone rings. You answer and someone tells you that when you turn twenty-one, you'll inherit a million dollars. Sweet, huh? You can't touch the money now, of course. But the promise that it's coming gives you hope.

When you become a follower of Jesus, you have an inheritance, one even better than a million dollars. It's the promise of heaven. You can't touch it now, of course. But the promise that it's coming gives you hope. Hope that helps you look up instead of down when circumstances are tough. Hope that helps you do what is right even when you're tempted to do what is wrong.

The inheritance God promises won't fade, rust, or wear out. The hope of that is meant to sustain you today. Yes, today might be hard, but remember it isn't forever. Your inheritance is coming!

*Jesus, thank you for hope that lives inside of me. When
I get wrapped up in what's around me, remind me of the
inheritance you have for me.*

OCTOBER

Let the beauty of the LORD
our God be upon us,
And establish the work
of our hands for us.

PSALM 90:17 NKJV

GIFT OF GUILT

For day and night your hand was heavy on me; my strength was sapped as in the heat of summer. Then I acknowledged my sin to you and did not cover up my iniquity. I said, "I will confess my transgressions to the LORD." And you forgave the guilt of my sin.

PSALM 32:4-5 NIV

Did you know that feeling guilty can sometimes be a gift? Not a general, vague sort of guilt but the kind of guilt you feel after you've done something wrong. That sinking inside your stomach when you know you've done wrong. That restlessness inside that bothers you so much, you can't stand it.

Guilt is a gift because it's a gentle reminder to make right what is wrong. For example, if you've spent the morning complaining to your mom about having to do your homework and then feel bad because you know she's just trying to help, that "feeling bad" is a good thing. It's God way of encouraging you to change your approach from complaining to gratefulness and to make things right with your mom.

Instead of stuffing the guilt or trying to forget about it, confess what's wrong—to God and to the person you've wronged. Then enjoy being in right relationship with both of them.

Father, thank you that you've made a way for me to be in close relationship with you, even when I sin. Remind me that I never have to run and hide, only confess and be restored.

LIVE WISELY

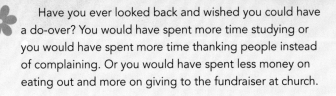

So teach us to number our days,
That we may gain a heart of wisdom.

PSALM 90:12 NKJV

Have you ever looked back and wished you could have a do-over? You would have spent more time studying or you would have spent more time thanking people instead of complaining. Or you would have spent less money on eating out and more on giving to the fundraiser at church.

You only live each day once, so make it count. That doesn't mean party up, but live each day in a way that you won't regret. In the scheme of all eternity, your time on earth is incredibly short. So make decisions with eternity's values in mind. Make your life count!

Father, as the Psalmist prayed, I ask you to remind me to make the most of every day and to live wisely.

WHAT YOU EAT

I could not address you as people who live by the Spirit but as people who are still worldly—mere infants in Christ. I gave you milk, not solid food, for you were not yet ready for it. Indeed, you are still not ready.

1 CORINTHIANS 3:1-2 NIV

When a baby is born, he or she can only eat one thing—milk. No burritos, no steak, no smoothies, no potatoes. Just milk. But as babies gets older and their digestive systems mature, they can begin to enjoy other foods, like corn on the cob, or chef salad, or a big piece of pizza. Those foods make them grow and thrive. If they tried to live on just milk, they wouldn't have enough energy to get through the day.

This is the analogy Paul makes. He calls the adult Christians "infants." That's not a compliment. He wishes they were more mature. Instead they are still drinking milk.

What are you eating? Are you able to chew on the difficult areas of following Jesus and obey, receive his loving discipline, and give him all you have? Or are you like an infant who can't handle all that a mature Christian can? God isn't looking for instant maturity, but he does want commitment to taking steps in that direction.

Jesus, I want to be a mature Christian, someone who isn't caught up in small, worldly things. Help me to dig deep into your Word, to know you well, and to be open to correction.

A JONAH

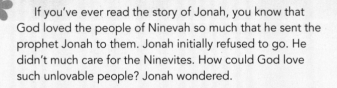

Should I not have concern for the great city of Nineveh, in which there are more than a hundred and twenty thousand people who cannot tell their right hand from their left?

JONAH 4:11 NIV

If you've ever read the story of Jonah, you know that God loved the people of Ninevah so much that he sent the prophet Jonah to them. Jonah initially refused to go. He didn't much care for the Ninevites. How could God love such unlovable people? Jonah wondered.

While it might be easy to judge Jonah, ask yourself if you've ever done the same. Do you find it hard to love those that God has put around you? Admittedly, the people that need Jesus the most are often the most unlovable. They might be offensive, annoying, or just plain mean. But unless they hear about and are shown God's love, they might be lost forever. That fact should overcome any reluctance you have to tell them about God.

The people in your life are not there by accident but rather by design. You have the opportunity to point them to Jesus. Pray for them, ask God to have mercy on them, and take every chance you can to share the Lord with them.

Holy Spirit, help me see others the way you do and love in such a way that points them to you and not away from you.

INCAPABLE OF FAILURE

*God so loved the world that he gave his one
and only Son, that whoever believes in him
shall not perish but have eternal life.*

JOHN 3:16 NIV

The word "love" can mean different things depending on the person who says it. Has anyone told you they loved you and then stepped out of your life as quickly as they came in? Has anyone ever said they loved you in one breath and then mistreated you in the next? Has anyone ever claimed to love you when really they should have used the word "lust"?

Humans have an extraordinary ability to fail each other, even if they mean well. God is altogether different. When he says he loves us, we can't assume he'll fail us like everyone else has. His love doesn't fail or falter; it's steady, strong, and consistent. The depth of that commitment and love was shown through Jesus. God loved us so much that sent his only Son, Jesus, to die so that we could have eternal life.

Father, thank you that your love will not fail me. Instead of beating myself up for my weak love for you, help me fall into your arms of steady, unfailing love.

IN THE LOVE OF GOD

Keep yourselves in God's love as you wait for the mercy of our Lord Jesus Christ to bring you to eternal life.

JUDE 1:21 NIV

How frustrated do you feel when you tell people something and they refuse to believe you. That's how God feels when he tells you he loves you and you question him. "If God really loved me, then this bad thing wouldn't have happened," you might say. Or, "God says he loves me but I've messed up so badly."

Despite what you might think, God loves you deeply. And he knows that his love is intended to be your very lifeblood. Knowing God loves you will be the primary force that sustains you through rejection, suffering, and loneliness. His love is perfect. It isn't manipulative or self-serving, but pure. You also play a part in this great love. You can choose to reject it or accept it. God tells you to remain in his love, wanting you to have all the benefits it brings. Don't run from it.

God, help me to believe in the depth and height and greatness of your love for me. When you discipline me, help me remember that you are doing it for my own good. Your love never fails.

PERSISTENCE PAYS OFF

*Jesus told his disciples a parable to show them
that they should always pray and not give up.*

LUKE 18:1 NIV

You hear a knock at the door but you're busy and can't get to it right away. The knocking gets louder. "I'm coming!" you say. But whoever is knocking doesn't hear you, and they start banging louder and faster. "Just a minute. I'm coming!" you say again. Finally you swing open the door. If you were even considering not opening the door, you'll finally give in because of the constant knocking.

If you read the parable in Luke 18, you'll understand that that's how Jesus encourages us to pray—with persistence. God doesn't always answer prayer right away. That's not because he's not listening. That's not because he's reluctant to answer and is toying with your feelings. Wait for his timing. In the meantime, don't be discouraged. Keep praying, and don't give up.

*Lord, teach me to be persistent when I pray. I know you
don't always answer right away, but I know you listen and
you care.*

BELIEVE

"Do not let your hearts be troubled. You believe in God; believe also in me."

JOHN 14:1 NIV

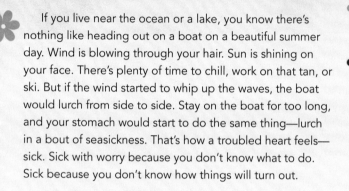

If you live near the ocean or a lake, you know there's nothing like heading out on a boat on a beautiful summer day. Wind is blowing through your hair. Sun is shining on your face. There's plenty of time to chill, work on that tan, or ski. But if the wind started to whip up the waves, the boat would lurch from side to side. Stay on the boat for too long, and your stomach would start to do the same thing—lurch in a bout of seasickness. That's how a troubled heart feels—sick. Sick with worry because you don't know what to do. Sick because you don't know how things will turn out.

Jesus knew that you'd feel troubled at times. So he gives you this reminder—believe.

While it's so much easier to *do* something, the best approach you can take is to trust. Believe that God's got your back. Believe that he knows what's going on. Believe that if you ask for wisdom, he'll answer.

God, I spread my prayer requests out before you, and I wait for you to answer. When I begin to doubt, give me the faith to believe that you are big enough to solve my every problem.

HIGH QUALITY

God demonstrates his own love for us in this:
While we were still sinners, Christ died for us.

ROMANS 5:8 NIV

The difference between a Coach purse and a knock-off at the local mall is quality and cost. A Coach purse has a high cost that comes with prestige. Because of that cost, it's highly valued by the person who bought it.

You were bought at an extremely high cost. That's proof of God's love. God loved you so much he sent Jesus to die on the cross so you could have forever life. It's also proof of your value to God. He wouldn't have paid such a high price if he didn't think you were worth it. God chose you. He wanted you as his child. He was willing to initiate the relationship with you and pay whatever price it took to ensure that you had the opportunity to become a daughter in his kingdom.

Father, thank you that you were willing to pay the price for me to enter your kingdom.. Thank you for valuing me and loving me.

HOW TO PRAY

*Once Jesus was in a certain place praying. As he finished,
one of his disciples came to him and said, "Lord,
teach us to pray, just as John taught his disciples."*

LUKE 11:1 NLT

Prayer is simply talking to God. Sometimes simple things
can seem difficult. Maybe you don't know what to say to the
one who made you. You're not alone. The disciples asked
Jesus to show them how to pray too.

The Lord's Prayer is a great template or pattern for
learning to talk to God. First recognize that God is the
perfect Father. He loves you! Praise him. He is holy and
good. Then ask him for the things you need. Deal with any
unconfessed sin and receive his forgiveness. After you have
dealt with sin, go enjoy him! Thank him, listen to him, and
appreciate his affectionate listening ear.

*Lord, teach me how to pray. I get sidetracked so easily. I
forget that you enjoy my company and you like to talk to me.*

IN NEED OF A FATHER

You have not received a spirit that makes you fearful slaves.
Instead, you received God's Spirit when he adopted you
as his own children. Now we call him, "Abba, Father."
ROMANS 8:15 NLT

When Jesus taught his disciples to pray, he started by teaching them to call God "Father." This is a significant difference from other major religions. Other gods have a god-servant relationship. God invites people into a personal relationship with him—that of a parent and a child. He remains holy and set apart, but at the same time invites each person to draw close to him. So close that they can call him "Abba," a term little children used for a father they trusted completely.

You may have grown up without a father or with a poor example of one. Because of this, when you hear God call himself Father, it may cause you to recoil. Realize that God isn't like a human dad. He is altogether perfect and his fathering heart toward you is flawless.

God, thank you that you invite me to call you Abba. Thank you that you are not ashamed to call me your own. Help me trust your love more and more.

ATTACKED

*We are not fighting against flesh-and-blood enemies,
but against evil rulers and authorities of the unseen
world, against mighty powers in this dark world,
and against evil spirits in the heavenly places.
Therefore, put on every piece of God's armor.*

EPHESIANS 6:12-13 NLT

Sometimes you are doing everything you can to obey God, and you still feel like you are getting hit from all sides. This is because we do not just wrestle with flesh and blood. Satan and his demons do have power and influence on the earth. When sin entered the world, it brought disorder where there was once peace.

While that is a fact, it shouldn't scare you. God has given you instructions on what to do when you feel attacked. James 4:7 says first to submit yourself to God. That's right. Don't proudly try to solve your own problem: submit to him. Then resist him and he has to flee! Not because you are great but because God's Spirit lives inside you and *he* is great.

Praise you, God, that victory is yours. You've promised that, as your daughter, I can resist the devil and he has to flee. There is no one as strong, powerful, and mighty as you who fights for me.

NEVER UNLOVED

That you, being rooted and grounded in love, may
have strength to comprehend with all the saints what is
the breadth and length and height and depth, and to
know the love of Christ that surpasses knowledge.

EPHESIANS 3:17-19 ESV

"He loves me; he loves me not."
"He loves me; he loves me not."

Insecurity can plague us during the teen years. We wonder, What does that person think of me? They say they like me, or even love me, but do they really? There's one person's love that you can absolutely count on—God's. One of the surest paths to walking in greater security is being rooted and grounded in love. That just means understanding how deeply God loves you. Knowing someone loves you gives you confidence. That confidence is so deep it can't be stolen when others are unkind to you.

God's love for you is the purest and strongest love there is. It is greater than a slow dance on prom night, a kiss in the hallway, or a romantic proposal. As you meditate on this love of God, all other likes or loves pale in comparison. You, dear one, have never been unloved!

Father God, thank you for choosing me and welcoming me
into your family. No one can love me the way you do. Help me
not to look other places for something only you can provide.

THANKFUL FOR LIFE

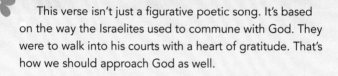

Enter his gates with thanksgiving;
go into his courts with praise.
Give thanks to him and praise his name.
PSALM 100:4 NLT

This verse isn't just a figurative poetic song. It's based on the way the Israelites used to commune with God. They were to walk into his courts with a heart of gratitude. That's how we should approach God as well.

You may wake up with a heavy heart, feeling like you want to give up on your day. Instead, you can choose to thank God—for his provision, for his love, for the life he gave you. If you do that, whether you feel like it or not, you'll soon find that your heart feels lighter. Talking to God should be your first line of offense in tackling an unwanted day. Instead of beginning to pour out all your complaints to God, discipline yourself to praise him.

Father, thank you for life and breath. Today help me to pause and remember all that you have done for me.

A PERFECT PLAN

*The LORD makes firm the steps of the
one who delights in him.*

PSALM 37:23 NIV

There are certain privileges that come with being a daughter of the King. Namely, you will live forever in his kingdom. Another privilege is having the opportunity to find out the perfect plan God has for your life. You simply don't have the big picture that God does. You don't see all that he sees or know what he knows. So any steps you plan to take are limited by what you know and what you see.

Because God though is aware of everything and knows you intimately, he is capable of leading you into a beautiful plan. Humility says, "God, I know you know me better than I know myself, so I choose your plan for my life." If you follow his lead, the Lord will make your steps certain and firm.

Father, thank you that I am yours. I want to humble myself before you, knowing that it's a decision I'll never regret.

WHERE TO TURN

When doubts filled my mind,
your comfort gave me renewed hope and cheer.
PSALM 94:19 NLT

Worry, worry, worry. There are hundreds of things you can choose to worry about in a day. What will they think if I wear this? What if I gain weight? What if I don't get accepted into the college I want? With thoughts like these, your anxiety level will shoot through the roof. It will steal your joy and peace.

The psalmist in this verse was once overwhelmed with worry. But he gives an answer to getting through it—going to God for comfort. That means you don't go somewhere else for it. When you do, it only treats the symptoms, and that kind of comfort won't last. Go to God with your worries and anxieties because he knows the source of your pain. His love takes away your fears and fills you up with joy.

Father, show me any unhealthy ways I might be trying to cope with anxiety. I want to turn from them and instead turn toward you: toward your comfort and the joy it brings.

MEDITATION

Happy are those who don't listen to the wicked,
who don't go where sinners go,
who don't do what evil people do.
They love the Lord's teachings,
and they think about those teachings day and night.

PSALM 1:1-2 NCV

We hear a lot about meditation these days. But what does it really mean? In many religions, it means to empty one's mind and achieve a kind of higher consciousness. For followers of Jesus, meditation means filling one's mind with God's Word and regularly thinking about him.

Making a habit of memorizing God's Word and thinking on what God has to say can have a huge impact on your life. You'll find that during the day, when you need it the most, a verse might pop into your head giving you direction and wisdom. And when you've got down time, instead of worried thoughts popping up, you'll find verses being brought to mind.

Father, help me develop the habit of meditating on your
Word so I develop positive patterns of thinking. Help my
actions to follow my mind that is devoted to you.

EARN A GOOD DAY

LORD, *every morning you hear my voice;*
Every morning, I tell you what I need,
and I wait for your answer.

PSALM 5:3 NCV

If you've grown up in a church setting, you've likely been told to spend some time with God every day. Some people refer to this as a "quiet time" and others call it "devotions." Perhaps that is why you are reading this book right now—because you are having devotions for the day.

Spending time talking and listening to God every day is a great lifelong habit to create. However, just because you have taken the time to meet with God doesn't mean you earn a great day from him. In fact, devotions aren't meant to earn you anything. Spending time with God is meant to get you in the habit of talking and listening to your Father. The more you talk to him and study his Word, the easier it will be to hear him during the day, on rough days, happy days, and days when you need some help.

Thank you, Lord, that you hear my voice in the morning and all throughout the day. Help me set aside time each day to talk with you.

NIGHTS

In peace I will lie down and sleep,
for you alone, LORD, make me dwell in safety.
PSALM 4:8 NIV

Sometimes children get fearful in the evening before going to bed. In their little world, when night comes and they can no longer see well outside, fear sets in. They might need multiple reminders from their parents that they are safe and secure. Even when kids get older, while they might stop crying out to their parents at night, the fear is still there.

It seems that even King David in the Bible wrestled with nights. But it's clear David knew there was one reason that he could both lie down and fall asleep in peace—God was keeping him safe. It wasn't the Israelite armies that made him safe. It wasn't the weapon by his bedside that made him safe. It wasn't the palace guard that kept him safe. It was God.

That same God who kept David safe is the one keeps you safe as well. Call on him and know that he will stay awake, guarding you while you sleep.

Father, thank you that you stay awake all night long. Please cover me and protect me so I can dwell in safety.

A LIFE OF DEPENDENCE

For this reason, I am happy when I have weaknesses, insults, hard times, sufferings, and all kinds of troubles for Christ. Because when I am weak, then I am truly strong.
2 CORINTHIANS 12:10 NCV

What makes an alcoholic an alcoholic or a drug addict a drug addict is extreme dependency. That person needs alcohol or drugs in order to function and doesn't know how to operate without them. In some ways, people with addictions have half the equation right. They understand their need for something stronger than themselves. Where they go wrong is in choosing what they depend on.

We were actually all *designed* to live lives of dependence. Everyone has a built-in need to lean on someone who is much stronger than they are—God. When we are weak, we have the opportunity to depend on him, to draw close to him. We can lean on him, the one who is strong enough to handle all our pain, weaknesses, hurts, and questions.

Lord, help me remember that when I am weak, I have the opportunity to depend on you. You are strong when I'm weak.

THIRSTY

My soul thirsts for God, for the living God;
When shall I come and appear before God?
PSALM 42:2 NASB

God designed your body to need food and drink. Eating and drinking gives you the physical energy you need to function throughout the day. To stop eating and drinking means getting thirsty, hungry, and eventually dying.

The same is true for your soul: it needs to be fed and watered as well. This kind of eating and drinking means spending time with the Father. It means letting him love you. It means turning to him and learning his Word. It means sitting in his presence and listening to his voice. When you neglect this regularly, you allow restlessness, insecurities, and fears to take hold in your heart. Make a habit of "feeding" your soul so you'll grow spiritually strong.

Father, remind me to come and feast at your table daily: not to prove my spirituality to you, others, or myself, but simply because you invite me to spend time with you.

SECRET SINS

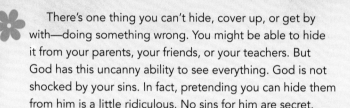

You have set our iniquities before you,
our secret sins in the light of your presence.
PSALM 90:8 NIV

There's one thing you can't hide, cover up, or get by with—doing something wrong. You might be able to hide it from your parents, your friends, or your teachers. But God has this uncanny ability to see everything. God is not shocked by your sins. In fact, pretending you can hide them from him is a little ridiculous. No sins for him are secret.

Because he knows and loves us, God made a way for us to deal with sin. It's actually quite simple. The Bible teaches us to confess our sins. That just means admitting we're wrong. Then we're to accept the forgiveness God gives. That's an act of faith. He offers it; we believe it. So rather than try to hide what is impossible to keep a secret, come clean with God and embrace the forgiveness he offers.

Lord, thank you that you have made a way for me to be free
from guilt and shame. Today, I confess those sins that I've
kept hidden so I can receive your forgiveness. Amen.

NO MORE SHAME

Indeed, none who wait for you shall be put to shame.
PSALM 25:3 ESV

We hear a lot about how Jesus forgives us and frees us from guilt. But do you know that Jesus also takes away shame? Shame tags along with sin. On the outside you might look confident, but on the inside you're filled with deep regret because of something you did. A sense of shame can also come from people—people who speak cutting remarks or treat you like you're not measuring up, you're a mistake, or you're an embarrassment.

When Jesus died on the cross, he took away *both* your guilt and any sense of shame. Stay close to God and hear what *he* has to say about your value and worth. Other voices are silenced when he says, "I forgive you. I love you."

Father, thank you that you never intended for me to live in shame. Through your love and the power of what Jesus did on the cross, free me from any sense of shame.

NOT OVER YET

He who testifies to these things says,
"Yes, I am coming soon."
Amen. Come, Lord Jesus.
REVELATION 22:20 NIV

Turn on the TV or your smart phone these days and all that seems to come up is a string of discouraging news. Between news about wars, famines, modern day slavery, and natural catastrophes, it's hard not to have a heavy heart. It might seem like the times we are living in are getting darker and darker. And in many ways, they are.

But the best news is this: things aren't over yet! Jesus prophesied in Matthew 24 that many difficult things would happen before his return. You can have hope that Jesus is coming back. He'll have the final say and will make all things new. Ask God to open your eyes to the ways he's working around you. While evil sometimes *seems* to be winning, grace is at work everywhere.

Dear Lord, thank you that you have the final say in the world around me. Help me to keep my eyes open for the good things you're doing every day and to keep hoping for the day when you'll return.

ARGUING WITH GOD

Who are you, a human being, to talk back to God? "Shall what is formed say to the one who formed it, 'Why did you make me like this?'"

ROMANS 9:20 NIV

Imagine you're creating a bowl out of wet clay when all of a sudden the clay starts to argue with you: "Hey, why are you making me into a bowl? Shouldn't you be making me into a plate? And if you're going to make a bowl, there are a lot better ways to do it, you know."

It sounds a little ridiculous, but that's often what we do with God. There's no end to his wisdom and knowledge, yet we argue with what he's doing all the time.

God can handle your arguments. They don't threaten him or make him insecure. However, they aren't accomplishing anything in your heart. You have to remember that God knows what he is doing. He has the benefit of the big picture, beginning to end. You don't. It's in times like this that you simply need to trust him. He won't fail you and he promises to make things come together for good.

Father, thank you that you know what you are doing. Help me to trust you when I don't agree and don't understand.

BEST YEARS

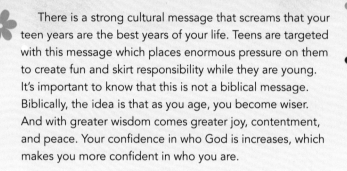

Blessed are those whose strength is in you,
whose hearts are set on pilgrimage.

PSALM 84:5 NIV

There is a strong cultural message that screams that your teen years are the best years of your life. Teens are targeted with this message which places enormous pressure on them to create fun and skirt responsibility while they are young. It's important to know that this is not a biblical message. Biblically, the idea is that as you age, you become wiser. And with greater wisdom comes greater joy, contentment, and peace. Your confidence in who God is increases, which makes you more confident in who you are.

Viewing your life as a pilgrim on a long journey is much more accurate than thinking all your best days come first and then it's downhill from there. As you walk this journey with God, your trust of him increases. You will be amazed at the places he takes you. Hang in there. The best is yet to come.

Father, give me the courage to resist the lies of our culture.
I am on a journey with you, and I thank you for all that is to
come, not just the years of my youth.

HOW MANY DAYS

*Teach us to number our days
that we may get a heart of wisdom.*

PSALM 90:12 ESV

When you are young, aging seems like...well that it is ages away! Rationally, you realize that you will age someday, but that almost seems like an abstract concept. Because of this, it is easy to buy into the message of YOLO. You feel the liberty to make terribly unwise decisions because you reason that at some point, when you are older, you will fix any mistakes you made in your youth.

The truth is you have no idea how long you have on this earth. "Numbering your days" is an expression that means you choose wisely what you do every day because you aren't guaranteed the next. There is great wisdom in striving to live each and every day with purpose. Let the Lord use your days to bring him glory.

Father, I pray that I would be wise beyond my years. Help me live with purpose and intention now and not assume that I will be able to later. Help me gain a heart of wisdom in my youth.

IN THE BEGINNING

In the beginning, God created the heavens and the earth.
GENESIS 1:1 ESV

"Ma-ma. Da-da." Those are some of the first syllables a baby learns. They serve as the building blocks of everything to come. Soon those syllables turn into words and words into sentences and sentences into complete and complex ideas. The first verse in Genesis spells out the foundation of everything else in the Bible. God existed before the creation of the world; the world was conceived by him. What an amazing thought! It's something that should inspire awe and worship.

Unfortunately instead of that truth, we hear the opposite. We hear that there is no Creator and the earth came into being on its own. "In the beginning" there was no God, people say. With that attempt to paint the first foundational truth as a lie, the door is opened to questioning the rest of God's Word as well.

Precious one, stay grounded in this truth: in the beginning, God created the heavens and earth.

Father God, you created the world and everything in it, including me. I'm in awe of who you are and all you've done. I praise you!

NOT MOODY

He never changes or casts a shifting shadow.

JAMES 1:17 NLT

Anger. Jealousy. Love. Sadness. These are emotions we all feel at one time or another. What we often don't realize is that God feels all these emotions too. He felt frustrated and angry at the Israelites' constant complaining. He was jealous of the idols they worshiped. Other times, God was so happy he felt like singing.

The difference between God's emotions and ours is that his are not whimsical or unpredictable. He doesn't change like shadows that shift over the course of a long summer day. He may feel different emotions at different times, but those emotions are always consistent with his love. His love is constant, stable, and secure. When others around us seem inconsistent, we can have peace and a sense of security that the stability of God brings.

Father, thank you that your character never changes. I can always count on your love.

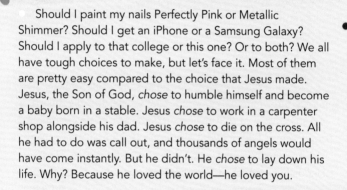

TOUGH CHOICES

*"No one takes it from me, but I lay it down of
my own accord. I have authority to lay it down,
and I have authority to take it up again. This
charge I have received from my Father."*

JOHN 10:8 ESV

Should I paint my nails Perfectly Pink or Metallic
Shimmer? Should I get an iPhone or a Samsung Galaxy?
Should I apply to that college or this one? Or to both? We all
have tough choices to make, but let's face it. Most of them
are pretty easy compared to the choice that Jesus made.
Jesus, the Son of God, *chose* to humble himself and become
a baby born in a stable. Jesus *chose* to work in a carpenter
shop alongside his dad. Jesus *chose* to die on the cross. All
he had to do was call out, and thousands of angels would
have come instantly. But he didn't. He *chose* to lay down his
life. Why? Because he loved the world—he loved you.

The only way it was possible for you to have a
relationship with a holy, perfect God was for your sins to
be forgiven and taken away. And that could only happen
through sacrifice and the blood that Jesus shed. He knew
that only through his death could you have life. So, next
time you're faced with a tough choice, remember the one
who loved you and made a huge choice for your good.

*Thank you, Jesus, for willingly laying your life down for me. I
am so grateful for your sacrifice. Help me love you in return.*

MAKE ME CLEAN

God made him who had no sin to be sin for us, so that in him we might become the righteousness of God.

2 CORINTHIANS 5:21 NIV

Have you ever gotten a stain on your favorite jeans or favorite top? You could spray it with stain remover, soak it in cold or hot water, or just throw it right into the washing machine. Even then, sometimes that stain just won't come out. It's time to throw those clothes out.

Sin stains our lives permanently. When we do something wrong, there's nothing that can take that stain out—except the blood of Jesus. That's the only thing that has the power to remove sin (Hebrews 9:22). God goes a step further though. When we ask for forgiveness, not only does he give us forgiveness, he also gives us the righteousness of Jesus. It's like getting a brand new pair of clothes: clothes of righteousness.

Father, please take my shame and guilt away. Would you wash away the stain of sin and clothe me with righteousness?

NOVEMBER

Take delight in the Lord,
and he will give you your heart's desires.
Commit everything you do to the Lord.
Trust him, and he will help you.

Psalm 37:5 nlt

DESIGNED FOR HONOR

You are precious to me. You are honored, and I love you.

Isaiah 43:4 ESV

Sometimes we wear clothes because everyone else is wearing them; other times it's because they are comfortable. Sometimes we aren't even aware of how we are dressed. It might not have ever occurred to us that our bodies were designed to be honored and beautiful.

God, your Maker, speaks of you adoringly and places tremendous value on you. You are precious to him. Maybe you haven't been treated that way by others. Maybe you've felt the need to draw attention to yourself in ways that reveal more of you than you want. Attention, though, doesn't equal love. Love is pure and self-sacrificing. There is no one who will love you as purely as your Father in heaven. Dress like the precious person God created you to be.

Father, help me to see me as you do. Help me receive your love, so I don't look everywhere else for it.

WHAT TO WEAR

"Seek the Kingdom of God above all else, and live righteously, and he will give you everything you need."

MATTHEW 6:33 NLT

If you have a date or are going to a prom or a wedding—even just arriving on the first day of school—you've probably thought a lot about what you were going to wear. Believe it or not, God knows you like to look good.

Jesus said, "Look at the lilies of the field and how they grow. They don't work or make their clothing, yet Solomon in all his glory was not dressed as beautifully as they are. And if God cares so wonderfully for wildflowers that are here today and thrown into the fire tomorrow, he will certainly care for you" (Matthew 6:28-29). Solomon was the king of Israel. You can be sure that he had a closet full of clothes.

Worrying about clothes, worrying about what people think of your clothes, and spending too much time and money on them are signs that they've become too important. What's most important is seeking God and living right. If you do that, he'll take care of the clothes part of life.

Father, help me to set my eyes and my heart on more important things than what I wear. Please remind me to seek your kingdom first.

RIGHT DISCIPLINE

*Blessed is the one you discipline, LORD,
the one you teach from your law.*

PSALM 94:12 NIV

When you hear the word *discipline*, what emotion comes to mind? If discipline was done in a loving way, perhaps you feel respect. A parent who disciplines well communicates that the discipline is for their child's good. If discipline was abusive or carried out in anger, maybe the emotion that comes to your mind is anger or fear.

Parents aren't perfect, but God is a perfect Father. The discipline he gives is described as a blessing. In other words, it is a gift from God to you. God, who sees better than anyone else, loves you by giving you boundaries and kindly and firmly disciplining you when you step outside them. Why? Because he knows that outside them, you'll get hurt. The best place, the perfect place, is smack in the middle of his ways. If God is saying no to you, *trust him* and submit to him. It is for your own benefit.

God, thank you that I can know you're a good Father because you discipline me when I'm wrong. Help me to see the discipline you give as a gift and a sign of your love.

GREATER THAN FEAR

*I prayed to the Lord, and he answered me.
He freed me from all my fears.*

PSALM 34:4 NLT

Is there something you are afraid of? Perhaps you've never shared this fear with anyone else but it pesters you constantly. It may be a debilitating fear that wraps you up so tight you feel like you can hardly breathe. You might not even know where the fear came from. Others might think it's unreasonable. Fact is, though, you're afraid.

God knows you are wrestling. He sees your fear and he sees you. He wants to deliver you from it. First, ask God when the fear first crept into your life. Next, ask him to forgive you for anything he shows you that you've done wrong. Lastly, ask him to place a protective barrier between you and that fear. Then thank him that fear doesn't have any power over you—he does. You can be sure that God wants you to be free!

Father, you're greater than my fear. Please free me from the fear that is troubling me so much. Thank you for listening and answering my prayer.

FULL LIFE

"The thief comes only to steal and kill and destroy; I have come that they may have life," and have it to the full."
JOHN 10:10 NIV

Have you ever had a supposed "friend" who said and did all the right things while around you but behind your back was completely different? Our enemy, the devil, is a lot like that. He's a two-faced liar whose ulterior motive is to steal, kill, and destroy. He sets out to destroy lives and relationships, steal peace and joy, and kill any chance of people enjoying a sweet relationship with God.

Jesus Christ, on the other hand, longs to give life—*full* life. Where the enemy steals, kills, and destroys, Jesus gives, builds up, and encourages. He brings courage, joy, peace, and a sense of confidence.

God, thank you for the life you give. Help me be alert to anything that isn't from you.

GOOD FRIENDS

Blessed is the one who does
not walk in step with the wicked
or stand in the way that sinners take
or sit in the company of mockers,
but whose delight is in the law of the LORD.
PSALM 1:1-2 NIV

Think over the last week. Who did you spend most of your time with? Who did you talk with on the phone? Who did you sit with at lunch? Who did you hang out with when you went to the mall? Taking a look at those you're spending time with is really important. That's because the people you hang out with impact the type of person you become. If your friends cheer people up, work hard, and treat people well, it will subconsciously encourage you to do the same.

If your friends criticize, gossip, or complain, it'll rub off on you. That's not to say you shouldn't be a friend to these people or be a friend to those who don't know the Lord. But they shouldn't be your closest friends. Spend time with people you want to be like—friends whose delight is to love God.

Father, give me friends who will help me be more like you
and will build up my faith.

ROOTS

*They are like trees planted along the riverbank,
bearing fruit each season. Their leaves never
wither, and they prosper in all they do.*

PSALM 1:3 NLT

Scripture often compares Christians to plants or trees. Both have roots that sink deep into the ground. The roots of a plant or tree are its stabilizing force. It doesn't matter how tall the tree or plant grows above ground, if the roots are grounded and secure, the plant won't topple over.

As a believer, we have roots too. Our roots are the foundational truths that come from Scripture. One of those truths is found in Ephesians 3:17: God is love. As children of God, we need to be rooted and grounded in love. Not rooted in rules, tradition, or fear, but in love. Knowing that— really believing it deep down—will give you security and confidence.

You are loved. This should be the most foundational belief that you have about God. Everything else you hear about him or do for him should be built on this truth and this truth alone.

Father, I want to be firmly rooted in your Word. I want to be firmly rooted in your love. Reveal to me how much you love me.

STREAM OF GRACE

O Lord, you are so good,
so ready to forgive,
so full of unfailing love
for all who ask for your help.

PSALM 86:5 NLT

The Bible teaches that we have all sinned. There is not one believer in all of creation that has never sinned before God. Jesus is the only perfect man to have ever walked the earth. He alone bears the title of being the sinless one.

Because we have all sinned, we are in need of cleansing. God readily offers his forgiveness the moment one of his children cry out in repentance. He happily pours on a steady stream of grace and healing to the repentant heart. Sometimes, even after we have repented of certain sins, we still don't *feel* clean. But God wants you to know that no matter the extent your sin, upon your confession to him, he will make you clean. He is good and ready to forgive.

Father, thank you that your words have the power to make me clean after I have sinned. Please heal me and help me to walk closely to you so that I might hear your cleansing voice whisper, "You are clean."

HIS FRIENDS

"You are my friends if you do what I command you."
JOHN 15:14 ESV

In the United States of America, it is fairly common for people to call themselves Christians. The phrase "Christian Nation" gets thrown around so often that it almost makes us think if we are born here, we might naturally be Christians.

It's important to know how Jesus defines a Christian. After all, when you call yourself a Christian, you are saying you are a follower of Christ. In John 15, Jesus makes it clear that he wants his followers to be so close to him that he could actually call them friends. This is a crazy notion in some ways. Why would the God of the universe want to be friends with mankind? Because of his love.

We can't profess friendship to Jesus—through the title of being a Christian—and then live however we want. It's really quite simple: to be called a friend of God, we have to do what he commands.

Father, help me not love you with just my words but also with my actions.

NOVEMBER 10

SUBMISSIVE HEART

"I love the Father and do exactly what my Father has commanded me."

JOHN 14:31 NIV

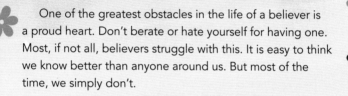

One of the greatest obstacles in the life of a believer is a proud heart. Don't berate or hate yourself for having one. Most, if not all, believers struggle with this. It is easy to think we know better than anyone around us. But most of the time, we simply don't.

There is a great litmus test to see if you have a proud heart or a submissive one. The Holy Spirit, who is quite intent on making you like Jesus, has a great way of setting up opportunities for you to deal with your proud heart. When you are in a situation where someone who has more power than you (e.g. parents or teachers) tells you what to do, you realize pretty quickly whether or not your heart is proud. Can you submit and do exactly what they have asked as Jesus did for his Father?

Lord, I confess my pride. Please help me to submit myself to those above me just like you did. I want to walk in your footsteps.

FATHER OF LIES

"There is no truth in him. When he lies, it is consistent with his character; for he is a liar and the father of lies."
John 8:44 nlt

Satan hates God with a fierceness that we can scarcely comprehend. Because of this, his favorite thing to do is to wreak as much havoc as he possibly can. Jesus is not intimidated by this. He teaches us how we should navigate Satan's actions on the earth. Satan is incapable of ever speaking the truth. He is the original source and the father of lies.

This is precisely why you have to closely watch your thoughts. Not every thought that flies through your mind is from you or God. Some are whispered by Satan. You don't need to fear though. As you grow in discernment and maturity, you will be able to realize that those negative thoughts are not coming from you. And if you know that, you don't have to feel guilty or dirty. Simply call on the name of Jesus, and invite him to help you take every thought captive and make it obedient to him. He will give you the grace to resist Satan's lies.

Father, thank you that your Spirit of truth is alive in me and will give me the strength I need to resist lies when they enter my mind.

PRINCE OF PEACE

He will be called Wonderful Counselor, Mighty God, Everlasting Father, Prince of Peace.

<small>ISAIAH 9:6 NIV</small>

Do you ever follow the news? Things can seem pretty bleak if you do. There are wars, famines, and stories of modern-day slavery that get reported frequently. If you listen to the suffering around the globe, it could be easy for you to lose your peace. It's true, we do live in an evil age. But that should not take away your peace. Your peace does not come from events but from a man—the Prince of Peace.

When Jesus shared some of his last teachings with his disciples before he was crucified, he told them how to love him unto the end. But he made it clear he wasn't teaching them those things to scare them. Instead, he wanted them to have the peace that only he had the power to deliver (John 16:33).

Father, thank you that you are our overcomer and the Prince of Peace. Please bring me the stability of your presence to give me the peace I need today.

PLAYING WITH FIRE

*Do not love this world nor the things it offers
you, for when you love the world, you do
not have the love of the Father in you.*

1 JOHN 2:15 NLT

We are warned throughout Scripture to watch out for sin. This isn't because God is mean. It is because he knows how damaging sin can be. It brings separation to the fellowship we are supposed to have with our Father, it opens us up to hear lies from the devil, and it makes us feel dirty.

God wants you to avoid sin because he loves you and wants to protect you. If you practice repenting quickly from your sin, it will not have a tight grip on you. But if you continue in it too long, you will learn to love it and not hate it as you should. When you love the world and all that it offers, you begin to steer away from the things of God. If this is the case, repent now, turn back and ask God to give you his heart toward sin again.

Jesus, I want to hate the things you hate and love the things you love. Please give me your Spirit so I can discern the difference.

REWARDS

*Anyone who comes to him must believe that he exists
and that he rewards those who earnestly seek him.*

HEBREWS 11:6 NIV

Our culture loves rewards. As children, we are often
introduced to reward systems. It's very simple. The giver
of the rewards makes it clear what needs to be done to
earn the reward. Often, there is a correlation between the
difficulty of what is being asked and the size of the reward.
The more difficult the task, the greater the reward.

We love this system because we were made for it. Our
Father in heaven loves rewarding his children. He sees every
single act of obedience that we make toward him, and he
knows exactly how much effort we put forth in obeying
him. This delights his heart, and he loves demonstrating
his pleasure through rewards. Some of his rewards will be
given to us on earth, but many are being stored up for us in
heaven. Don't doubt this truth.

*Father, thank you for your rewards. Give me long-term
vision to serve you well, knowing that you are watching and
rewarding my efforts.*

JUST PRAY

Then he prays to God, and is accepted by him,
he comes into his presence with joy,
and God repays him for his righteousness.

JOB 33:26 NRSV

It's easy to become overwhelmed by expectations. We want to fit in, to belong, but the formula is constantly changing, and it's hard to know whose standards we should shoot for: family, friends, school, work, social media…who decides what's acceptable?

Look carefully at the verse. What must we do in order to be accepted by God? Must we have our acts together, our sinful habits conquered, our church attendance perfect? No. Just pray. We pray to God, and he welcomes us in. Scrubbed and shiny or worse for wear, it's all the same to him. He sees you, he hears you, and he invites you into his joyful presence.

Father, help me to remember yours is the standard of acceptance that matters most, and that just by praying I've already met it. Thank you for loving me as I am.

DON'T HIDE

*Don't you see how wonderfully kind, tolerant, and patient
God is with you? Does this mean nothing to you? Can't you
see that his kindness is intended to turn you from your sin?*

ROMANS 2:4 NLT

A young girl stole from her grandmother one day. She
wasn't planning on it, and she didn't hate her grandmother.
It was simply that she was so tempted to take the money
that was sticking out of the purse, she couldn't resist. She
didn't even have a plan for the money; it just seemed to be
calling her name. The moment she grabbed it and put it in
her pocket, she regretted her decision. She wondered how
she could have been so foolish to steal from someone she
loved so much.

What the girl didn't know is that her grandmother had
seen the whole thing. But she was wise and she cared more
about the girl's heart than getting her money back. Instead
of demanding the money, she made her granddaughter her
favorite cookies. This random act of love and kindness was
enough to cause the girl to run into her grandmother's arms,
confessing her sin.

The grandmother in this story is but a dim reflection
of God.

*God, it's your kindness that leads me to repentance today.
Thank you for drawing me back to you with your whispers of
love and promises of peace.*

HEARING THE TRUTH

*"When the Spirit of truth comes, he
will guide you into all truth."*

JOHN 16:13 NLT

Do you have a steady habit of hearing truth? It's important to form that habit for a few reasons. It will give you wisdom where you lack it, freedom where you feel stuck, and peace where there is fear. The world will not speak truth to you. It will tell you you're ugly when you're beautiful, urge you to hold a grudge instead of forgive, and call "good" the things that are evil.

When you have a regular diet of hearing truth, you become quicker at discerning Satan's lies before they seep into your mind and heart. From free Bible audio apps, to worship music, to online sermons, you really have a buffet of options for hearing truth. Make the choice to put truth in your heart daily. You won't regret it.

*Father, give me the strength to pursue hearing truth
regularly at the expense of other habits.*

BROTHER'S KEEPER

"I do not know; am I my brother's keeper?"
GENESIS 4:9 ESV

One of the biggest distinctions of our faith is the way we are called to love one another. This is the way the world will know we are Christians. Take a second to break down what that means, so you can know how to accurately express it. It might mean forgiving someone who hurt you badly because you are also in need of forgiveness. It might mean being seen with your awkward church friend at school because love isn't full of pride. It might mean choosing not to wear the latest fashion trend because you know it could cause others to be tempted.

In Genesis 4: 9, we see the first picture of sibling rivalry. Shortly after Cain killed Abel, his brother, God came up to Cain and asked him if he knew where his brother was. Cain's response was opposite to what it should have been. He was supposed to love, protect, and honor his brother. That's what families do. We are family with those in the body of Christ. Let us love and keep each other well, so we might stand unashamed before God.

Father, please show me how I can be better at loving my brothers and sisters in you. I want the world to see your love through my love for your body.

A PROTECTIVE DAD

The LORD God made garments of skin for
Adam and his wife, and clothed them.
GENESIS 3:21 NASB

While they are becoming few and far between, some of the best movies highlight a loving relationship with a father and his daughter. When a movie depicts a dad protecting, loving, or sheltering his little girl, it's hard not to have a misty eye as we watch. It is the picture we all long for.

There truly is no better example of protective love than that of the Father toward his creation. One only needs to read the first three chapters of the Bible to see this love on display. After Adam and Eve sinned in the garden—consciously, willfully and blatantly—they quickly learned the consequences of their sin. But God also communicated his protection of them by taking time to cover their nakedness and assuring them of his plan for restoration.

Father, thank you that you are the kind of dad who will clothe me when I need covering. You protect me. Today, once again, I submit to your authority and lovingkindness.

A CHILD'S SONG

Jesus loves me this I know,
For the Bible tells me so.
Little ones to him belong;
They are weak, but he is strong.

It's probably the most popular Sunday school song. Church children grow up hearing it almost from birth. And those who have never attended church also seem to be familiar with it. It's a simple song but absolutely foundational to our faith.

You are loved. The Bible illustrates that better than any other book. It reveals God's plan for redeeming the earth through Jesus. He goes to extravagant lengths to save us and win our hearts. Read your Bible. It will remind you of God's love when you feel unworthy, alone, or when your heart is tempted to look elsewhere for love and acceptance.

Father, thank you for your love demonstrated in your Word.
Draw me to your Word and reveal your love to me again.

CATCH A GLIMPSE

*"He will wipe every tear from their eyes, and
there will be no more death or sorrow or crying
or pain. All these things are gone forever."*

REVELATION 21:4 NLT

To a certain extent, you were made to know the future.
Not just to have an educated guess as to what it would look
like, but to have a confident, accurate picture of what reality
will one day be. The earth is groaning and waiting for Jesus
Christ's return. He came once as a baby, grew up, and died
here. But he will come again. And this time his body won't
be broken. It will be his strong, resurrected body that is
incapable of tasting of death. When he returns, he will make
all the wrong things right.

Jesus will establish his Kingdom on the earth. Why does
he go into such great detail about removing our sadness?
Because our sadness grieves him. It wasn't meant to be this
way. God is more eager than you are to wipe your tears
away. That day is coming. Catch a glimpse of it today and
allow it to give you the strength and the courage to press on.

*Father, I long for your return. Fill me with reminders that you
are coming, so I can press forward with hope in this age of
suffering.*

JUST A TASTE

Taste and see that the LORD is good!
PSALM 34:8 ESV

A dieting mother was often known to ask for a taste of her children's treats—whether it was an ice cream cone, a warm cookie, or a brownie smeared in frosting. She didn't think she could allow herself to have an entire serving, but a simple taste would indicate to her whether the treat was as good as it looked.

God challenges you to taste his goodness as well. It is an invitation to experience for yourself what you have heard. In some ways, this verse almost reads like a dare. God is so eager to pour his goodness on you, but you have to stick out your tongue and try it. He isn't going to smash the ice cream cone in your face to prove it's good. Take him up on his offer. You won't be left in want.

Father, help me experience your goodness first hand and not just read about others who do. Today, I choose to taste and I trust that as I taste, I will then see just how good you really are.

PRE-EXISTENT

In the beginning was the Word, and the Word was
with God and the Word was God. He was with God
in the beginning. Through him all things were made;
without him nothing was made that has been made.

JOHN 1:1-3 NIV

God the Father wasn't the only one present when the earth was created. There were two others there as well: the Holy Spirit and Jesus. It's a beautiful picture that we won't fully grasp this side of eternity. But God exists in three separate persons, and those three expressions of God have existed from before there was time.

Jesus' existence didn't begin the day he was placed in Mary's womb. He has always been and will always be. He is the beginning and the end. Sometimes it's hard to grasp what God might actually be like because he is so different from us. When you wrestle with that, just look to Jesus. He is the exact representation of God (Hebrews 1:3). If you want to know how God acts, feels, and responds to his children, then study the actions, tears, and words of Jesus.

Jesus, thank you that you have always been there and will always be there. I trust you. Please reveal the Father to me that I might adore you more.

STRENGTH AND JOY

Splendor and majesty are before him;
strength and joy are in his dwelling place.

1 CHRONICLES 16:27 NIV

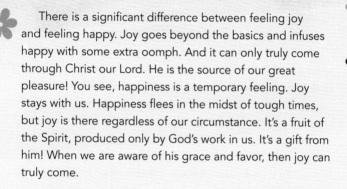

There is a significant difference between feeling joy and feeling happy. Joy goes beyond the basics and infuses happy with some extra oomph. And it can only truly come through Christ our Lord. He is the source of our great pleasure! You see, happiness is a temporary feeling. Joy stays with us. Happiness flees in the midst of tough times, but joy is there regardless of our circumstance. It's a fruit of the Spirit, produced only by God's work in us. It's a gift from him! When we are aware of his grace and favor, then joy can truly come.

Experiencing the Lord's joy doesn't mean you'll never feel sadness again. Hard times come to everyone regardless of our maturity in faith. Pray that you will feel great pleasure in your life no matter what comes your way. Put your trust in him. He loves you, and wants to share all of his gifts with you.

Thank you, God, for the strength and joy that come from being with you. No matter what comes my way today, I can choose joy because you are with me.

WAITING FOR JUSTICE

"For I, the LORD, love justice;
I hate robbery and wrongdoing.
In my faithfulness I will reward my people
and make an everlasting covenant with them."

ISAIAH 61:8 NIV

It's not fair! How did she get away with that! We have all thought that before when someone hurts us or is dishonest about something and doesn't get caught. Sometimes things are unfair, and it's hard to ignore them. We want justice, and we want it now!

There is a lot of injustice in this world, and it can be frustrating, sad, and confusing to think about. There is hope. God teaches us in his Word that he is just. He sees and knows it all. He is quick to love and slow to anger, but those who hurt his children and do not repent will be punished.

Lord, sometimes I have a hard time waiting for justice. Help me to be merciful toward others and let you do the work of justice. You will make everything right in the end.

A GOOD LEADER

*"I am the good shepherd. The good shepherd
lays down his life for the sheep."*

JOHN 10:11 NIV

What do you look for in a leader? If we are to bring
others into a relationship with Christ, we are all called to
become leaders ourselves. One of the best examples we
could ever ask for in leadership was Jesus himself. And he
called himself a good shepherd. There was good reason
for this. Though a shepherd, at the time, was not a job
that many aspired to, it called for special skills. A shepherd
had to guide his flock of sheep without scaring them into
submission. Sheep are known to make poor choices when
operating under fear.

Shepherds needed to nourish, comfort, lead, correct,
and protect their sheep. And most importantly, a good
shepherd would encourage those in their care to follow his
example and stay with him. Are you a leader for Christ's
kingdom? Are you encouraging others to follow your
example, comforting them in times of need and correcting
them gently when the situation calls for it?

*Lord, please help me to display good leadership in my life.
I want to model myself after you, the good shepherd, and
care for others by leading them to you.*

WALKING IN OBEDIENCE

Blessed are all who fear the LORD,
who walk in obedience to him.

PSALM 128:1 NIV

Why is obedience to God so important? Simply put, our obedience is a demonstration of our love for him. Though good works don't give us eternal salvation (only a relationship with Jesus can do that), if we truly love God, then we have a desire to follow him and live a life of good deeds. We will want to follow the example set by Christ and live our lives modeled after him.

There are times when everything in us wants to rebel against what we're told to do—whether it's to clean our rooms, stay away from bad influences, or turn homework in on time. But a life in Christ is one that is transformed. It may not be easy, but it is possible to begin to desire to walk on the path God sets for us.

God, when I feel like rebelling, help me to set that feeling down. Change my heart so I will desire to walk in obedience to you.

FINDING REST

"Submit to God and be at peace with him;
in this way prosperity will come to you."
JOB 22:21 NIV

Did you know that God designed our bodies to require rest? It seems like a luxury to have rest in this day and age, and the ability to truly enjoy it becomes difficult. Our minds begin to think about the things that we need to get done, or perhaps we get distracted by other people and things clamoring for our attention.

Like a car that needs to be filled with gas and have the occasional oil change to operate correctly, our body, mind, and spirit need peace and rest to operate well. The peace that God wants to give us is a supernatural peace. It's a peace that feeds us in all areas of our lives and restores our souls. All that is required of us is to recognize that we need his peace, and then to take the time to slow down and meet with him.

God, whether it's an hour on the couch, or a quick prayer and a deep breath in the hallway at school, help me to seek you first and not as a last resort after total burnout. I want to find my rest in you.

A MARATHON LIFE

We are surrounded by a great cloud of people
whose lives tell us what faith means. So let us run
the race that is before us and never give up.
HEBREWS 12:1 NCV

If you are an athlete, then you know what it means to persevere. Pushing yourself past your wall, breaking down what you thought were your limits, and hanging on to the end are all a part of an athlete's way of life.

Our lives as Christians are like a marathon. There is the world's greatest prize waiting for us if we can push through and endure until the end. When we cross the finish line, we get to run into the arms of Jesus. Hardship will come, but we can get through it if we just keep our eyes on that prize.

Lord, help me keep my eyes on the prize—eternal life with you. Help me through the tough times and give me the ability to persevere. I know the prize waiting at the end is worth it!

WINTER

*For everything there is a season, a time
for every activity under heaven.*

ECCLESIASTES 3:1 NLT

God did something remarkable when he created seasons. If you live in an extreme climate, you have likely observed this. How can the same tree be so full of vibrant green leaves one moment and then completely barren only months later? In winter, you can hardly see any signs of life in its branches and trunk unless you look closely. The tree is indeed alive; it is just dormant. That same tree will once again produce promising buds that will give way to rich, hearty leaves.

You are not very different from a tree. In fact, God compares us to trees and plants often in Scripture. There will be seasons that it seems you are bearing tremendous fruit in your life. You feel fresh and alive. But there will also be seasons, like winter, where your branches appear to be dead. Fear not, dear child. God is still at work, and he promises that you will bear much fruit again.

Father, help me trust that you are working, regardless of the season I am in. Give me faith and hope to remain in you.

DECEMBER

Oh, the depth of the riches

both of the wisdom and

knowledge of God!

How unsearchable are

His judgments and

unfathomable His ways!

ROMANS 11:33 NASB

FAITHFUL WITHOUT FAIL

Let us hold firmly to the hope that we have confessed,
because we can trust God to do what he promised.

HEBREWS 10:23 NCV

Did you know that the Lord is always faithful? He is! Always, without fail, he will follow through on what he tells us. Though there may be times when our earthly eyes have a hard time spotting him working in our day-to-day lives, he is always there. He has promised to be faithful to his children, and he will never go back on his Word.

So press on. Live in hope for your future and all the beauty that is ahead of you. Be confident in what he says. Hold on to your expectations for a life to come. Don't give in to the temptation to see only what's here and now. Keep your eyes on the future hope that eternal life provides.

God, help me to keep my eyes fixed on you and the
promises you have made. When I struggle to see what's
happening now, I remember your Word and look to the
beautiful future ahead of me.

DWELLING ON TRUTH

Listen, my dearest darling,
You are so beautiful—
You are beauty itself to me!
SONG OF SONGS 4:7 TPT

Do you ever hear voices in your head that tell you you're not good enough? Do you need others' approval and opinions to give you confidence? There is good news: you are enough! God made you just the way he wants you. Those voices in your head that say you're not good enough are lies.

You can do anything God calls you to. When the voice of discouragement comes, silence it. When you find yourself desiring approval, shift your thinking and seek God for confidence. What God thinks of you matters the most.

God, the more I practice dwelling on the truth, the more I will see how valuable I am in your eyes. I want you to define me and be proud of who that is.

AN IDEAL OUTCOME

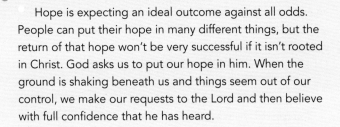

*I pray that God, the source of all hope, will fill
you completely with joy and peace because you
trust in him. Then you will overflow with confident
hope through the power of the Holy Spirit.*

ROMANS 15:13 NLT

Hope is expecting an ideal outcome against all odds.
People can put their hope in many different things, but the
return of that hope won't be very successful if it isn't rooted
in Christ. God asks us to put our hope in him. When the
ground is shaking beneath us and things seem out of our
control, we make our requests to the Lord and then believe
with full confidence that he has heard.

Placing our hope in the Lord begins with giving him the
desires of our heart and then truly trusting him with those
desires. He honors the hope we have in him and he knows
how weak our hope can be. Sometimes it's scary to place
great hope in someone for fear of being disappointed. This
is where we need to trust and accept that our loving Father
knows what is best for us. If we hope for something that is
not to our benefit, then he won't grant our request—and we
will be better for it!

*God, I hope and trust in you. I know that you want what will
bring me closer to you. You hear my requests and lavish me
with your love.*

MEASURED WORTH

*Whether, then, you eat or drink or whatever
you do, do all to the glory of God.*

1 Corinthians 10:31 NASB

Too often we measure our worth based on what we do. We label ourselves because it gives us a sense of self-importance: *I am an honor student. I am a star athlete. I am a ballet dancer.* We all have a need to know why we wake up in the morning, so we cling to labels as if our lives depend on them. If our current situation does not meet our expectations, we feel worthless and insignificant.

The good news is that we all have purpose that cannot be measured: young or old, teacher or student, mother or daughter, doctor or janitor. If we live for God, we are exactly where God wants us to be, doing exactly what he wants us to do. We don't have to go on an extravagant crusade, earn straight A's or don ballet slippers to find our purpose. Our purpose is to love God, abide in him, know him, and serve him. We just have to embrace it.

Father, thank you that I don't have to try to figure out what my life's purpose is. I have purpose right where you have placed me. My life is significant and valuable because it is found in you.

ADORED

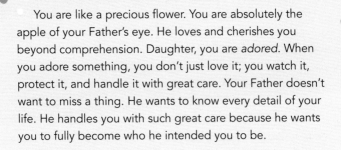

"You are a people holy to the LORD your God.
The LORD your God has chosen you to be a
people for his treasured possession, out of all the
peoples who are on the face of the earth."

DEUTERONOMY 7:6 ESV

You are like a precious flower. You are absolutely the apple of your Father's eye. He loves and cherishes you beyond comprehension. Daughter, you are *adored*. When you adore something, you don't just love it; you watch it, protect it, and handle it with great care. Your Father doesn't want to miss a thing. He wants to know every detail of your life. He handles you with such great care because he wants you to fully become who he intended you to be.

Because God adores you, he sometimes allows you to go through some things that don't feel good. But God is perfect. He is good, loving, and protective. You can trust that in those difficult moments, he is shaping and molding you to be more like him.

God, I want to believe that you adore me, and that I am a richer person because of the difficulties you have allowed to cross my path. Thank you for your goodness in those moments and for loving me completely.

EQUIPPED TO CONQUER

I remind you to fan into flame the gift of
God... for God gave us a spirit not of fear
but of power and love and self-control.

2 TIMOTHY 1:6-7 ESV

Any new situation can be daunting. A new school. A new job. A new group of friends. A new adventure. A new opportunity. Any of these could cause our knees to buckle and our hearts to race. Sometimes we need boldness for the concrete and tangible fears we face: an angry family member, a disgruntled friend, a failed test. Maybe we need boldness to defend the weak and rise up for the forgotten. Sometimes we simply need boldness to do what we know is right.

Many times, we want to cower and hide, but hiding doesn't make fears disappear. Instead, they are allowed to fester and grow. Before we know it, fear is taking control of our lives. You may wish that you were braver. You *can* be. God has equipped you with everything you need to conquer any situation. He has given you the weapons to fight with—chin up and shoulders squared. You never have to go into any situation afraid. You can have full assurance that God will give you the boldness you need in the exact moment you need it.

God, you made me a warrior. Warriors don't run from scary situations; they march forward and battle on. Show me just how brave I can be when I depend on you.

357

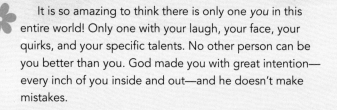

ONLY ONE YOU

*The LORD will be your confidence and will
keep your foot from being caught.*

PROVERBS 3:26 ESV

It is so amazing to think there is only one *you* in this entire world! Only one with your laugh, your face, your quirks, and your specific talents. No other person can be you better than you. God made you with great intention—every inch of you inside and out—and he doesn't make mistakes.

You are beautiful in God's eyes, and he created you for a purpose. The only way you can fully accomplish his purpose for your life is to get to know yourself and accept the beautiful person you are. When you do this, you wear an outfit called *confidence*. It's the kind of clothing that shines bright and attracts others to its light.

Lord, reveal to me more of who I was created to be. Thank you that there is a mission for me in life: to love and accept myself for who I am. Help me to be me because nobody else can do it better!

SIMPLY DELIGHTED

"The LORD your God in your midst,
The Mighty One, will save;
He will rejoice over you with gladness,
He will quiet you with His love,
He will rejoice over you with singing."

ZEPHANIAH 3:17 NKJV

Did you know that the mighty God, creator of heaven and earth, is a proud Papa? That's right! He is a loving Father who delights in you—his child! He created you not just so you can enjoy him, but so he can enjoy you. Every good thing that is in this world is from God and teaches us about his character. Humor and laughter, art and creativity, peace and quiet, and excitement and surprises: all are a part of who he is. There are many things that he enjoys, but we are at the top of his list.

God delights in the way you see things, the sweet thoughts you have, the things that make you laugh, and the way you represent him. He delights in your hard work and determination. He adores you because he made you. You are his.

Thank you, God, that you love me and nothing can change that. Help me to be encouraged by that today.

A CHOICE IN ANGER

*"Don't sin by letting anger control you." Don't
let the sun go down while you are still angry.*

<small>EPHESIANS 4:26 NLT</small>

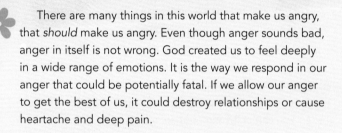

There are many things in this world that make us angry,
that *should* make us angry. Even though anger sounds bad,
anger in itself is not wrong. God created us to feel deeply
in a wide range of emotions. It is the way we respond in our
anger that could be potentially fatal. If we allow our anger
to get the best of us, it could destroy relationships or cause
heartache and deep pain.

In our anger we always have a choice. We could lash out
and be destructive, or we could allow our anger to evoke
change in an unjust situation. It is possible to feel angry,
yet exercise restraint and self-control when encountering
unpleasant or unfair circumstances. We can take comfort
that God knows how we are feeling in every moment—in
every situation—and that he cares deeply.

*God, help me choose to be loving and grace-giving
when I feel as if my anger is spiraling out of control.
Thank you that you don't abandon me in my emotion.*

WOMAN OF DIGNITY

She is clothed with strength and dignity;
she can laugh at the days to come.

PROVERBS 31:25 NIV

When Proverbs 31 describes the perfect woman, one of the key ways she is described is as being dignified. What exactly does that mean? It's having pride in who you are, and it's a quality that commands respect. God calls us to clothe ourselves in dignity, to wrap ourselves up in it so completely that we become the very essence of the word.

Take a look at your life and your day-to-day actions. Do you believe that the way you are presenting yourself to the world is respectful? As you get dressed, envision yourself first putting on dignity. Wrap yourself up in it before you head out for the day.

Lord, help me in my endeavor to be clothed in dignity and grace. I desire to bring honor to your name as I go about my day.

MEASURE OF SUCCESS

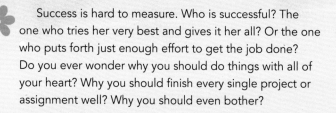

*The plans of the diligent lead to profit
as surely as haste leads to poverty.*

PROVERBS 21:5 NIV

Success is hard to measure. Who is successful? The one who tries her very best and gives it her all? Or the one who puts forth just enough effort to get the job done? Do you ever wonder why you should do things with all of your heart? Why you should finish every single project or assignment well? Why you should even bother?

Nothing good comes out of not trying your best. There's no success or sense of pride and accomplishment. There is no reward in cutting corners. Who wants to be known for their lack of attention to detail, their careless ways, or lazy, half-hearted attempts? Being diligent every day takes a lot of effort and energy. It also takes discipline. But through it all, your character is being shaped and strengthened. Even if the reward isn't immediate, the day will come where you will be able to see the fruit of your labor.

Lord, help me to be diligent in every task even if my efforts go unnoticed. Let my completed work be a reflection of my desire to honor you in all I do.

DONE WITH EXCELLENCE

*By his divine power, God has given us everything we
need for living a godly life. We have received all of this
by coming to know him, the one who called us to himself
by means of his marvelous glory and excellence.*

2 PETER 1:3 NLT

When we think about doing things with excellence, we
think of doing them to the best of our ability. To excel is to
never stop or settle for less, but always grow and get better.

Excellence is what the Lord desires for us—in our walk
with him and our attitudes toward others. He desires us to
have a hunger to pursue him and a heart that is willing to
be taught by him. When things are done with excellence,
whether in music, sports, friendships, studies, or otherwise,
we have an understanding that there is always more to learn
and achieve. This is the attitude our Father wants us to have
regarding our walk with him.

*God, I don't want to settle for "good enough." I want to
go forward in life, always putting my heart and mind in a
position to learn and grow. Thank you for helping me do
things with excellence.*

THANKFUL FOR FAMILY

My child, listen to your father's teaching
and do not forget your mother's advice.
Their teaching will be like flowers in your hair
or a necklace around your neck.

PROVERBS 1:8-9 NCV

If someone were to take a group of people all different ages and genders, put them in a house, and say, "Okay you are a family now, so get along, and love each other!" it would be incredibly difficult. It may even be a disaster. Thankfully, that is not the way families are designed. Family is created by God. He designed each of us a certain way and thought very hard about which family we would belong in.

When we are placed in a family, whether through birth or adoption, we are specifically chosen by God to be placed right where we are. Each person within the family is a gift. That's right! Your sister that wears your shirt without asking is a gift. That little brother that totally embarrasses you in front of your friends is a gift too. It is important to look at each member in our families as a gift from God. Each of us helps the other grow. Maybe that annoying little brother was put there to help us with patience, or the sister who took that shirt is teaches us to be less selfish. God knows where he wants to take us, and training is needed before he sends us out.

Thank you, Lord, for my family: my own personal training ground. Help me to continue to be thankful for each person you have placed in my family.

STRANGLING FEAR

"Be strong and courageous. Do not fear or be in dread of them, for it is the LORD your God who goes with you. He will not leave you or forsake you."

DEUTERONOMY 31:6 ESV

Some people are afraid of spiders, others are afraid of the dark. Fears are not uncommon, but we don't usually like talking about them. Sometimes we don't share our fears because we are embarrassed or because we feel like we will look weak and silly. But if we bottle up our fears, they have the tendency to grow into huge obstacles that are challenging to overcome.

Fear has a way of strangling our hope and courage. It can keep us from living a free and joy-filled life. It can keep us from pursuing our dreams. It can even keep us from making wonderful friendships and experiencing new things. Fears can grip us if we don't give them over to God. God is our light in the scariest of places. With him by our side, we can face whatever causes us to be afraid.

God, I lean on you today and ask for your help. Give me a boldness like I've never known before. I know I can conquer my fears with you at my side.

GOAL OF PEACE

A gentle answer deflects anger,
but harsh words make tempers flare.
PROVERBS 15:1 NLT

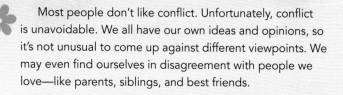

Most people don't like conflict. Unfortunately, conflict is unavoidable. We all have our own ideas and opinions, so it's not unusual to come up against different viewpoints. We may even find ourselves in disagreement with people we love—like parents, siblings, and best friends.

In the heat of an argument, it is tempting to bite with our words. But fighting doesn't resolve anything; in fact, it only makes the situation worse. Words are powerful: we shouldn't let them flow free without thought. Our hearts in every conflict should have peace as the end goal. We may not ever come to full agreement, but we can resolve every conflict with gentleness and love.

Father God, help me to be gentle. I want to put myself in someone else's shoes and show them kindness even in moments of conflict. Thank you for your grace. Help me to extend the same to others.

SHOWING GRATITUDE

*I, with shouts of grateful praise, will sacrifice
to you. What I have vowed I will make good. I
will say, "Salvation comes from the LORD."*
JONAH 2:9 NIV

When you're young, your parents give you constant
reminders to use good manners. One of the most popular
phrases in a growing family is, "Say thank you!" There's a
reason why parents want to teach the lesson of showing
gratitude. There is simply nothing better than doing
something for someone and knowing that they are thankful
for it.

So we thank our friends for a ride, thank our grandma for
a birthday gift, and thank someone for having us over for
dinner. But when was the last time you thanked God for all
that he's done for you? Our Father in heaven wants to know
you are thankful for your many blessings too. Even Jonah,
sitting in the stinky, dark belly of a giant fish, showed his
gratitude to the Lord. If Jonah can be thankful from the pit
of a fish, we can be thankful for all that we have.

*Thank you, God, for all the blessings you have bestowed
upon me. I am truly grateful.*

DEVOTED IN LOVE

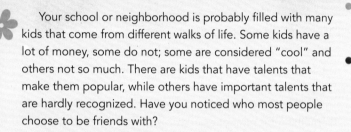

*Be devoted to one another in love. Honor
one another above yourselves.*

ROMANS 12:10 NIV

Your school or neighborhood is probably filled with many kids that come from different walks of life. Some kids have a lot of money, some do not; some are considered "cool" and others not so much. There are kids that have talents that make them popular, while others have important talents that are hardly recognized. Have you noticed who most people choose to be friends with?

When we think about Jesus and his friends, we remember that he befriended the underprivileged, the tax collectors, and the not-so-popular. When these individuals got to know Jesus as a trusted friend, they felt honored and loved for who they were. He honored others above himself. Because of this, their lives were forever changed. It is easy to honor, love, and be friends with those that are like us, but it is Christ-like to look for those who may need a friend and make them feel loved and respected by honoring them above yourself.

Lord, please show me if there are people in my life that I need to give more honor, love, and respect to. I want to be devoted to others in love and start honoring them above myself.

MAGNIFICENT CREATION

*Generation after generation will declare
more of your greatness,
And discover more of your glory.
Your magnificent splendor
And the miracles of your majesty
Are my constant meditation.
Your awe-inspiring acts of power have everyone talking!
And I'm telling people everywhere
about your excellent greatness!*
PSALM 145:4-6 TPT

With technology and social media a click away, it's difficult to be inspired by the things God intended for inspiration. Minute by minute, our heads are down trying to connect with others. But what about the magnificent beauty that's also at our fingertips? God made us to be creative and he wants to inspire our creativity. That's why he gave us towering mountains, hand painted skies, starry nights, rippling rivers, amazing wildlife, and the changing of seasons. What he made was well thought out and it was all made with us in mind.

God knows we need his beauty not just to inspire us, but also to feed our spirits in a powerful way. He wants to meet with us in the quiet moments and teach us more about himself. It's in these sweet places that he wants to tell us he loves us.

God, I pray that I would be inspired by your creative gifts of beauty that are all around me. I am truly amazed by all you have created.

MAY IT COME TRUE

Mary responded, "I am the Lord's servant.
May everything you have said about me come
true." And then the angel left her.

LUKE 1:38 NLT

When Gabriel first announced to Mary that she would bear the Son of God, he said, "Greetings, favored woman! The Lord is with you!" (Luke 1:28) Besides the amazing news he brought, Gabriel made clear how highly God thought of her. Keep in mind Mary was a young teenager, still a girl. So she'd probably had doubts about herself. Maybe she'd had a few unkind things said to her by others. That's what makes her response so incredible.

How do you describe yourself? Are you self-critical? How about your teachers, your relatives? What do they say about you? Compare whatever they say with what God says about you. Decide today to let God's words and the positive words you hear about you be the truth. Join Mary in saying to God, "May everything you have said about me come true."

God, I am your servant. I pray that everything you say about
me, plan for me, and equip me to do come true.

IN AWE OF GRACE

*In him we have redemption through his
blood, the forgiveness of sins, in accordance
with the riches of God's grace.*

EPHESIANS 1:7 NIV

Have you ever seen anyone at a restaurant insist on paying for a bill twice? Not likely. Nobody in their right mind would pay for a bill that was already paid for in full, would they? It wouldn't make any sense. Yet we all fall into this terrible habit of reminding ourselves of our past mistakes and sins. We allow ourselves to be entrapped in what once was and forget that we are already redeemed. Our sins were already paid for. We are free and clear. Sin free. Debt free.

It doesn't matter who you were or what you did in the past. In God's love for you, in his mercy and grace, not only has he forgiven you, but he has redeemed you from a life of despair. He has taken what was once lost and broken, and transformed it into something beautiful.

Thank you, God, for clearing my history of sin. Help me to walk in freedom from condemnation and guilt. You took all that upon yourself so that I could live a new life. I am in awe of your grace.

HIS POWER

*Think clearly and exercise self-control. Look forward
to the gracious salvation that will come to you
when Jesus Christ is revealed to the world.*

1 PETER 1:13 NLT

Every day we face situations where we need to exercise self-control: in our attitudes toward others, especially when we disagree with them; with our friends when faced with peer pressure; with social media and maintaining healthy boundaries and time limits; with school assignments or commitments in making sure we try our best. Sometimes the pressure or expectation to have self-control can be overwhelming—especially when we are struggling with habits that are proving difficult to break free from. We might feel like we are at the mercy of our temptation.

The wonderful news is that we don't have to be controlled by our own desires, whims, or strongholds. We are not weak; in fact, God has made us strong. There is no need to become frustrated with our sin. Instead, we can hold our heads high and defeat whatever habit enslaves us or temptation that entices us because God has given us self-control. There is hope to be free from old patterns.

God, thank you for your power that lives in me. I can be free from old patterns because of that power. I look to you for self-control today, believing that you will answer me.

GLIMPSE OF LOVE

*Do not be lazy but work hard, serving
the Lord with all your heart.*

ROMANS 12:11 NCV

How many times a day do we see our hands but fail
to recognize their potential, their power, their ability? Our
hands can be used to bless many people around us. They
can wipe away tears. They can work. They can comfort. They
can *serve*.

There are many practical ways to serve those around
us. We could give our time to a lonely friend. We could
help a fellow student with their homework. We could buy a
meal for someone in need. We could spend an afternoon
cleaning our elderly neighbor's home, or visit a friend in the
hospital. These simple examples require a sacrifice of time.
In an act of service, we not only give a tangible gift, we also
allow others to catch a glimpse of God's love for them.

*God, you made me to love others. Help me serve those
you put in my path even when it doesn't seem rewarding or
pleasant. I know there is both joy and eternal blessing found
in serving.*

SUPERNATURAL STRENGTH

Do you not know? Have you not heard?
The Lord is the everlasting God, the
Creator of the ends of the earth.
He will not grow tired or weary, and his
understanding no one can fathom.
He gives strength to the weary and
increases the power of the weak.
Even youths grow tired and weary, and
young men stumble and fall;
but those who hope in the Lord will renew their strength.
They will soar on wings like eagles; they
will run and not grow weary,
they will walk and not be faint.
Isaiah 40:28-31 NIV

No matter how puny your muscles may seem to you, you are stronger than you know. You can do anything you set your mind to. And you'll do it because God gives you a supernatural strength to power through and endure.

God never wearies. He never gets too tired to help you make it through the worst the world can throw at you. Put your hope in him, and he will give you strength beyond your wildest imagination.

God, give me the tenacity to make it through the toughest of times. I know I can because you are with me.

JOURNEY OF HOPE

*"Look, the virgin shall conceive and bear a son,
and they shall name him Emmanuel,
which means, 'God is with us.'"*

Matthew 1:23 NRSV

The day had almost arrived! There were many people waiting for the birth of Jesus. The Jews had long awaited their Messiah, Mary and Joseph were waiting for their firstborn baby, and the Wise Men were looking for the sign. Jesus was the hope that they all looked toward.

There is always a journey involved in waiting for great expectations to be fulfilled. The Jews were preparing themselves for the appointed time, Mary and Joseph had to travel to another town, and the Wise Men had to follow the star. In our own lives, we sometimes forget that the journey is part of the fulfilment of the things that we hope for.

Are you waiting and hoping for something great to be fulfilled? Take a moment today to reflect on the journey of those that waited expectantly for their Savior.

*God, I pray that hope will remain in my heart
for what is to come.*

BLESSED

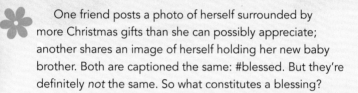

You honor me by anointing my head with oil.
My cup overflows with blessings.
PSALM 23:5 NLT

One friend posts a photo of herself surrounded by more Christmas gifts than she can possibly appreciate; another shares an image of herself holding her new baby brother. Both are captioned the same: #blessed. But they're definitely *not* the same. So what constitutes a blessing?

God's blessings are far more likely to come in the form of intangibles than brightly wrapped boxes. The Lord's riches consist of things like patience, mercy, grace, peace, and kindness. Jesus gives us truth, freedom, and light. The Holy Spirit brings love, joy, and kindness. Gifts are great, but blessings are divine.

Father God, help me this Christmas season to remember the difference between gifts and blessings, and guide my heart toward blessings. Fill me with your kindness, generosity and grace. Allow me to be a blessing to everyone I meet.

NOT WORTH WORRYING

"Can all your worries add a single moment to your life?"
MATTHEW 6:27 NLT

It's easy to worry about the future. How am I going to do on my test? Are we going to win that big game? What will she say when I confront her? Will I get that job? These are a few examples that can send our minds racing.

What is the point of worry? Has worry ever helped anyone feel better? Has it ever solved the problem? No. Everything that you walk through with God is not going to be easy, but worry does not have to be part of it. If you seek God during difficult times, you can have confidence that he has heard you, and he will work out his good and perfect will.

God, I ask you to take care of my concerns. Help me to let them go. I know I will not always get what I want, and I can't always make everyone happy. Let my focus be on pleasing you.

COMPLETE HEALING

He heals the wounds of every shattered heart.
PSALM 147:3 TPT

When we look closely at ourselves, sometimes all we see is a broken and shattered remnant of what we once were. Sin, tragedy, rejection, or heartbreak can leave us feeling terrible. We wonder how we can pick up the pieces and be made whole again. In our brokenness, it's easy to feel hopeless. We try different methods to fill the void. We may look to relationships, things, or drugs to fix us. They can make us feel better temporarily, but eventually we realize that despite all our efforts, we still feel broken and incomplete.

Who could possibly love and care for such a broken and tattered person? Jesus. He loves you. *All of you.* God is faithful. He doesn't leave you alone in your brokenness; instead, he meets you in that place, takes your broken pieces, and tenderly puts you back together again. Why? Because he loves you too much to leave you in the state you are in.

Father, help me find wholeness in you. You are the only cure for my pain. The best doctors and medicines can't provide what you do. Your love is so deep it can even remove my scars.

SHOES AND RIGHTEOUSNESS

"Where your treasure is, there your heart will be also."

MATTHEW 6:21 NIV

Clothing, shoes, popularity, and name brands are some pretty common things valued by teenagers. It's pretty difficult not to value these things yourself. But what has *true* value? God wants us to focus on valuing things that are of him— things like love, generosity, righteousness, and honesty. These things bring lasting value because they add to the kingdom of heaven. Clothing and popularity are temporary; they can be taken away or destroyed in a single day.

If you happen to be popular, or can afford those name-brand boots, that's fine, but the moment you find yourself being motivated by, and becoming focused on, those things, you have given them too much value. You can't place equal value on shoes and righteousness; it just doesn't work that way.

God, remind me that you are not impressed by name brands. You are impressed by the love you see in my heart, the honest words I speak, and the generosity I display. Help my heart to be focused on those things so that they are what I pursue.

WALKING IN TRUTH

Lead me by your truth and teach me,
for you are the God who saves me.
All day long I put my hope in you.

PSALM 25:5 NLT

When we think of truth, we often think of confessing something we've done that was not wise. But truth is also shown in the encouraging words we say to others and the life we live as representatives of God. Living a life for truth means to live in a way that stands for truth in all circumstances. It can be difficult to speak truth when there is a chance we may offend someone, be met with awkward silence, or stand with the minority.

You may find yourself in a situation where you feel the need to stand for what is right, but you're unsure you can find the courage to do so. Likely the Holy Spirit is nudging you to speak out in truth. If you listen to that nudge and obey it, you open a door for God to touch others. God loves when you stand for him, especially during difficult times. He sees what you do and say during those times, and it blesses him beyond measure to see your boldness for him.

God, as I continue to walk in truth, will you use me in great ways? I know you are preparing a beautiful place for me in heaven!

DESERT SEASONS

Trust the LORD with all your heart,
and don't depend on your own understanding.
Remember the LORD in all you do,
and he will give you success.

PROVERBS 3:5-6 NCV

There can be seasons where things don't seem to work out in your favor and life seems harder than normal. It could be issues related to relationships, school, sports, or even family dynamics. When things are tough in these areas, it tends to greatly affect our feelings, our mindset, and even our trust in God. We might feel like we're in the desert all alone.

The good news is that God knows just where we are. We are not lost. Many times when we are walking through difficult situations, the Lord has allowed us to experience those difficulties to test what is in our hearts. He is refining and maturing us. Though it may feel like he is far away, he's actually close by, molding and shaping us like a potter does with clay.

God, when I experience seasons of difficulty, I want to keep trusting you. Help me to be teachable so I can see what you want me to learn. Thank you that there is a purpose for my seasons in the desert. They allow me an opportunity to grow closer to you.

381

TOMORROW'S TROUBLES

"Do not worry about tomorrow, for tomorrow will worry about its own things. Sufficient for the day is its own trouble."

MATTHEW 6:34 NKJV

Many young people are overwhelmed and overbooked. Life is fast and it doesn't want to slow down for anyone. There are multiple assignments to complete, tests to study for, instruments and sports to practice, chores to do, and friends you need to keep up with. And if that's not enough, you may feel it all needs to be done with excellence.

Time out! When you are feeling stress creep into your life, it is important to get back to where God wants you to be. He wants you right next to him. He wants to gently walk with you and teach you how to look at stressors differently. All you can do is try your best and that is enough. Did you get that? Trying your best is enough. Nobody expects you to have super powers.

God, I want to spend more time with you so I can begin to see things through your eyes. When I do, I know it will be easier to accept that trying my best is enough. Help me to do just that in the coming year—try my best!